THE

FISHMONGERS

PETER WALMSLEY

Black Rose Writing

www.blackrosewriting.com

ISBN: 978-1-61296-190-3

PUBLISHED BY BLACK ROSE WRITING

www.blackrosewriting.com

Printed in the United States of America

The Fishmongers is printed in Cambria

For Jane

THE FISHMONGERS

To: Barbara,

Thank you for all your
support through this process.

Love,

[signature]

GLENN

Sunday was the day that my father flew the kitchen table. It was a large metal table with chrome and yellow enamel. Huge tubular legs, in tandem, anchored it to the floor. The yellow table top was suitable as a practice surface for the Toronto Maple Leafs. Metal chairs also painted yellow accompanied the suite. Making up the framing of these chairs were continuous chrome tubing which gave a little spring to the construction however, any comfort that would have been derived from the spring in the chair was negated by a flat pan like metal seat and metal backing. Although aerodynamically unstable the table flew quite well powered by Seagrams 83.

My mother flew as stewardess. Mixing drinks and providing necessary encouragement needed to make it to the next Seagrams and Pepsi. She would contribute to the conversations with poignant comments such as "Oh Glenn" and "Ah huh." Phrases that stood on their own merit.

Sometimes the kids boarded the flight but even a ten year old has limits to their imagination. Besides, there isn't a lot of room in a world war II vintage Harvard.

My father would regale us with stories of hardship during the war. Standing post, flying missions, lessons in navigation and all this under pressure of the theater of war as it took place at the flight training base in Montreal.

Glenn and Olivia had met at the Cub Flying School in Hamilton Ontario. He was a student pilot and she was a receptionist and typist at the school. She was a drop dead gorgeous, raven haired beauty and he was a thin, black haired, blue eyed good looking guy, dashing young pilot trainee. By all accounts they made quite couple.

After my mother's death my sisters were cleaning out her apartment and came across some letters that she had saved which clearly demonstrate that my Dad was head over heels in love with this gal.

February 8, 1944

Hello Sunshine

Well you gorgeous little doll another day has gone by, three to go "thank goodness" then I'll be back bothering you again with my sloppy lovemaking and cooing, my favorite pastime. How I love it. You're the cutest little fluff ball. I don't know what I would do without you? I might just as well not exist if you weren't around to look after me, love me, and well be my companion or is that the word for it, well anyway, be a part of me. Be in my every action and thought. Well you have the general idea of what I think about the whole affair or have you.

I will get a six thirty pass again this week darling, the sergeant said it's okay, not bad working in the office if it gets me the odd little favor now and then, and I don't mind at all, really I don't. Thank goodness somebody has a radio in this barracks at least we can listen to some music, I heard Bulldog Drummond last night. It was quite thrilling, it had me on the edge of the bed until it was over. Whew!

No letters yet honey I guess there will be one tomorrow though you don't know when you are getting mail around here. I think it's just when they decide to release it. I'm sure waiting for one believe me and it had better be a long one or look out, after all these nice long letters I send you I'm expecting letters back twice as long. (stinker aren't I darling).

Say honey, I just thought about it, I forgot to thank your mother for the snack we had Sunday night. Gorgeous, I love you with my whole heart. It will soon be Valentines

Day and I'm going to send you the biggest heart I can find and fill it with as much love as it will hold, just a little token to show you my love for you. That wasn't worded so good honey but we won't worry about that, as long as it gets the thought to you.

Well it's about time for me to hop up to my top bunk honey and dream about you and myself together for all times and never having to break up any more. It makes a wonderful dream honey and it's my favorite one. Good night darling.

Glenn xxxxx
(See you soon Sunshine)

And,

March 6, 1944

Hello Sunshine,

How are you keeping? I hope my little darling is in the best of health and looking as beautiful as ever. You know what honey? I love you, aren't you getting tired of me saying that wonderful, well even if you are I will still keep on saying it because I do love you darling with all my heart and believe me I'll really prove it to you in time. You know what time to dear, when there are no obstructions to hurdle and we are all alone in some hotel room away from home. Getting scared darling? I hope not.

I bet your folks laughed like mad when they saw we had opened our mickey after keeping it that long stored up in your cedar chest. I can just see your Pap now. By the way, darling, I didn't tell you in last night's letter, but I'm sorry for the dull evening you had and me being cross, honest I am honey.

I guess I talk too much business and not enough love

making. Please don't ever think that I don't love you darling. I will get down to some serious loving this weekend and let the marriage go along by itself. I guess everything will straighten out in due course. I'm just a damn old worry wart. By the way honey how's the war getting along pretty near over. I hope and pray and wish and everything else.

I'd love to have you here tucked away in my left hand pocket, just so I could take you out and kiss your precious little lips, give you a big hug whenever I wanted to. Boy that would be something to have you right beside me all the time instead of in my memory. Then when I went to bed at night I would wrap my arms around you, press you close to me and have your breath on my face all the time. What a dream I've got. I only wish it was true, and then I would really have something.

Well honey here I go again. I went in to here all about our weekend from the Major and the story is that we fly all weekend except if there is a change in orders. But in any case honey I will come home Saturday night because we will get that night off until eleven o'clock Sunday morning. I'm sorry sweetheart but that's the way it is at present. I am praying for a change of plans.

Well darling I hope I get a letter from you tomorrow and hear if you still love me. I hope.

This is about the end of my rope honey so I will say good night now and I will write you tomorrow night. I love you beautiful, look after yourself.

Glenn xxxxx

Meanwhile back at kitchen table aerodrome my Dad would grab hold of an imaginary "stick" and bring the engine up to revs, pull back the stick and achieve table rotation. After a short flight, perhaps to Malton Airport, he would ease the table back to the landing strip making a perfect landing on to the tiled floor. No doubt after a mission like that it was time for another rye and Pepsi.

Once gassed up again he would hum the RCAF anthem which sounded remarkably similar to the "Peter and the Wolf" tune. This would usually cause him to rise to attention and stomp his feet making, exaggerated right and left turns culminating with a snappy salute to some senior officer he had probably hated back in his days of the Royal Canadian Air Force.

Then the "I should have's" would start. "I should have applied to TCA. That's Trans Canada Airlines" he would add. "I'd be flying jet aircraft"

"Well why didn't you apply with TCA after the war?" someone would ask right on cue.

"Because there were too many pilots at the end of the war and they had the pick of the cream of the crop." Then it was my Mothers turn to assist with having him crash and burn, "You didn't even try. You just went back to work in the fish store with your mother and brother." The smoldering wreck of his dreams would lie there on top of the table. The table that just a few minutes ago had carried him into the clouds and back to his days of love and excitement. Back to a young man's unbridled belief in being able to do anything, with anyone and at anytime, for all time.

Yes the flights of fancy would continue through the afternoon fueled by rye and Pepsi until an overdone roast or some burnt bar b qued hamburgers would be served up for supper. Another Sunday would come to a close with my father going to bed early and my mother eating after everyone else had gone to bed.

THE FISH STORE

Edward Duncan had brought his family from England and crossed the Atlantic aboard the Canadian Pacific Steamship *Duchess of Bedford* arriving the Port of Montreal on July 9 1937. There was Bernia, his wife and sons Edward junior, aged 17 and Glenn, aged 15. They had no idea of what they would do for a livelihood. They settled in Hamilton Ontario. They consulted a lawyer who suggested that perhaps a fish or poultry business would provide for the family and from that City Fish and Poultry Ltd. was founded.

The store was on James Street close to the corner of Cannon Street. It was wedged between a drugstore and a men's clothing store. Above the store were apartments where the family settled in. An alley was accessible from Cannon Street that led to the back of the store where a large freezer unit as big as a garage stored the inventory. A wooden stair case gave access to the apartments. The alley, barely wide enough for a hand cart, was the main thoroughfare for carting the fish to the freezer from trucks that would park along Cannon Street.

From James Street looking in through the glass store front, there, displayed on gleaming white enameled metal trays were lobsters, whole fish, oysters, various assorted filleted fish, periwinkles , eels, octopus, crabs, every kind of sea creature and some you didn't know were represented to lure the fish buying customers.

Upon entering, one could not help noticing how immaculately clean this establishment was. There were refrigerated showcases made from Italian marble one inch thick. The glass fronts sparkled and in the cases row upon row of every type of fish imaginable stared back at you. In the far corner, available to the customer was a barrel full of shucked oysters. A ladle hung from the side of the barrel and little paper cones could be filled, for free, with oysters while you waited to be served. On the wall behind the showcases were shelves stocked with canned fish and jars of seafood sauce.

A porcelain clock hung on the wall that had its numbers replaced with EAT FISH OFTEN. Another sign hung on the wall reminding customers of the health benefits with the message. EAT FISH LIVE LONGER...EAT OYSTERS LOVE LONGER. At the back of the store facing forward was a small office designed to look like the pilot house of fishing boat. Wooden walls rose to support the windows of the land locked pilot house.

The business prospered, Edward and Bernia bought a house in the east end of Hamilton and upgraded to a home in Burlington just off of Lakeshore Drive. But somewhere along the immigrant success story Edward developed what has always been described as "shell shock." These were the days when if someone in your family had a mental disorder they were locked away in the attic. You didn't talk about it. So, no one talked about it. This was odd because he didn't have "shell shock" when he came to Canada. In fact he was a well respected business man in the Hamilton area. Upon his death the local paper ran a story about his contributions to the community. They told the story of how a down and out on his luck man was begging for a handout at the store one day. Edward asked the man why he didn't get a job. The man replied that he didn't have a descent suit of clothes and that because of that people wouldn't hire him. Apparently Edward abruptly took the guy next door to the men's clothing shop and had him fitted out with a new suit. The man got a job, became quite successful in his own right and never forgot what my Grandfather had done for him. This does not sound like the actions of a shell shocked individual. No, something else was going on.

My Father attended Cannon Street School and after his Father's death he left school to work in the fish store along side of his Mother and Brother. When the war broke out and conscription was invoked the rules allowed for one son to remain, where there was a widow involved, to work in the family business. My Uncle Junior, known as Junior, had no intention of leaving home or the business for war. Glenn was called up and told to report to the army. Having already amassed close to two hundred flying hours the army gave him twenty four hours to enlist in the Royal Canadian Air Force.

Glenn was accepted into the RCAF as a mechanic. In order to be given a flight status you needed a High School matriculation. He was back into the books and did two years of math, science and English studies in a matter of six months. He was accepted into the RCAF flight training school and reported to Fighter Flight Training School near Montreal.

OLIVIA

I used to think that my Mother must have come from a circus family. It was always difficult separating the bullshit from the facts. I suppose her early years were as close to a circus as it could be without actually living in a tent.

The Clark family, Samuel, Alma, Olivia and Emilia at first glance must have seemed as artistic and romantic as a Hollywood movie. Alma my Grandmother was beautiful and Samuel, my Grandfather, was larger than life. Their two daughters were about as cute as you could get without being illegal.

Samuel played saxophone in the big band era. He was in a band called the "Sundowners" and they played regular gigs around the Hamilton area. Samuel was also a sideman for big bands that would come up from the States.

Most big bands did not bring their entire personnel preferring to pick up local talent where they were booked to play. My Grandfather was a much sought after pick up player. He played with a lot of big names back in the thirties and forties. Jimmy Dorsey always tried to get my grandfather to sit in with his band when he was in town and stated in a local newspaper article that Samuel Clark was one of the best sax players he had ever had the pleasure to play alongside.

It was a big treat to have Gramps come on your birthday and play Happy Birthday on his sax. He was one of those "pull my finger" guys, sending us kids into fits of uncontrollable laughter when he would fart. I don't think my Dad got as big a kick out of his antics as we kids did.

Going up to my Grandparents apartment was something to look forward to.

They lived up on Aberdeen Street and all us kids would be crammed into the back seat of the family Pontiac singing from the moment we got in the car until we arrived, sung to the tune of

"Frere Jacques"; *"Aberdeen, Aberdeen, it's so clean, it's so clean.*

PollyWolly bingbang, Polly Wolly bing bang, Aberdeen, it's so clean."

I don't know what it means to this day but it rhymes and it was one of those things that would drive the old man crazy, which was probably the whole point.

The bathroom in my Grandparents apartment was a huge marble affair. The floor was white and black octagonal marble tiles. The walls were white marble tiles. The tub was a ball and claw porcelain and the room itself was huge. My Grandfather would sit on the can and practice his sax because he said the acoustics in the bathroom were great.

I remember once asking my Aunt Emilia what it was like growing up with grandpa and grandma, expecting to hear about how much fun it must have been. She told me "it was terrible." Her mom and dad fought like cats and dogs. My Gramps was an alcoholic who could never hold down a steady job. There was never enough money for the basics. They moved from one rented house to another. "But my Mom always talks about how great it was. That you guys were into gymnastics, singing and dancing. That gramps was a great father." "Your Mother is entitled to her interpretation" was all she said. My Mother was always into embellishing a story but I wondered how she could lose a grip on her own childhood situation. The two sisters were miles apart on this one.

Eventually gramps went to work at the fish store, invoicing, billing, general accounting and such. Dad gave him a job because he couldn't hold down a job; which helps to underline the level of qualifications required to work at the fish store.

There is no question that my Mom was quite a looker. Pictures from back in the forties portray a beautiful young woman. But people can fuck up anything. By the time she was in her mid thirties she was tipping the scales at two fifty maybe three hundred pounds. All five feet of her.

She never accepted responsibility for her body condition. She always blamed the birthing of her four children. "It was because of having you kids." She would lay that trip on us at every opportunity. And, for the most part, in our informative years, we believed her.

Most nights you could hear the television set down in the living room. Dad would have been off to bed hours ago, the kids were upstairs asleep in their beds, supposedly. The theme for the Johnny Carson Show would begin and like Pavlov's dog, Mom would be off to the kitchen. The great clatter of the cast iron frying pan as it would hit the stove top and the unmistakable sound of meat hitting the hot oil could be heard.

Mom bought a commercial freezer to help "stretch out the food dollar", so she said. It sat in the basement like a giant white coffin. It came complete with a lock. Now Mom was a pretty lazy gal and if she could get you to do something, like cross the room to get her an ashtray, turn up the TV, turn down the TV, she would. But one of the things she did not ask you to do often was get something out of the freezer for her. Once in a while, she would slip up and get you to retrieve some frozen peas or corn from the freezer. She would take the key that was on a chain around her neck and hand it to you as if she was lending you the Holy Grail. Now just hop down the steps and get me a bag of frozen cauliflower. Holy shit! There were steaks and roasts and juices and corned beefs and ice cream and all kinds of stuff that was never put on our table. You would bounce back up the stairs with some lowly fucking frozen cauliflower and ask her why we didn't get to eat some of those Shopsey's Corned Beef sandwiches. She would say "if you kids want me to get thin I have to eat that stuff." I'm sure, that if we had taken a vote, the kids would have opted for the Shopsey's Corned Beef sandwiches and to hell with Mom getting thin.

Instead of sharing in the tasty treats that lay locked away in the giant white treasure chest in the basement, we were treated to some of the worst food ever to cross a plate. We had stuff in our kitchen that didn't exist in the form it was originally purchased.

There were evolutionary discoveries to be made in our refrigerator. Best before dates were invented because of my Mom's kitchen.

One of her favorite meals, she never ate it, was boiled elbow macaroni. Now I would imagine after putting in a hard day reclined on a mattress and eating a pound of chocolate covered almonds one would think that they were entitled to a little loafing time. But that nagging question; what to feed the kids? keeps coming up. Having to crawl out of bed just before they come home from school, around four in the afternoon and thinking, what is a nutritious yet quick meal to set before my hungry little school warriors? Boiled elbow macaroni is the answer. Yes indeed! Boil up a whole package of that shit just in case they might ask for seconds. And when it comes to presentation don't forget the garnish, those little extras that make the meal so special. "My macaroni has ants on it!" I screamed in horror. "Those are poppy seeds... that's a garnish... you kids never appreciate any of the things I do around here. I try so hard to make things special... I don't know why I even bother."

Suspecting that there were ants on my macaroni did not come from out in left field. We had all had been introduced, face to face you might say, with Tapinome Sessile, the common house ant. Usually the little fellow could be found setting up housekeeping in our cereal. Mom would "stretch the food dollar" by purchasing a bulk bag of puffed wheat, approximately one hundred and fifty pounds at a shot. Whenever anybody asked me that stupid question "what weighs more a ton of feathers or a ton of steel?" I would answer "a ton of puffed wheat" and walk away. After filling you cereal bowl with puffed wheat and dousing it with milk you would merrily shovel this stuff into your mouth until you got to the milk line. That is where the last few puffs of wheat are floating in the bowl and that is when you would see them clinging desperately to sides of the bowl trying to get a foot hold. It looked like a scene out of the movie *A Night to Remember* where the remaining survivors have hit the water and are furiously attempting to climb into the already full life boats. The passengers inside the lifeboats begin to hit them with their oars in order to drive them off and keep them from swamping the boat. I didn't have an oar but I suppose the spoon worked just as well. When our Mother didn't get up to see her children off to school, which was almost always, a quick trip to the kitchen sink and what ants hadn't been used as a protein supplement to our diet were whisked down the drain. On the rare occasion when our Mother did get up, we always wished that she had not made the effort.

The morning would begin with our regular routine. Wake up and look under the bed for something to wear. Come down stairs having not washed or brushed your teeth or performed any act of hygiene, nor would we.

Get a bowl, get a spoon, get the puffed wheat and get the milk, sit down and put the puffed: her bedroom door would open and we would look at each other as if we were to be immediately devoured by some hideous giant troll. A thunderous slapping sound resonated throughout the kitchen as her road packer feet would hit the tiled floor. Looking like a poorly trimmed main sail she would waddle to the table in one of her polyester, semi-transparent negligees coming to rest in one of the metal chairs. Having settled, she would heave her pendulous breasts on to the table. Her areola's staring out at her children like some predator seeking revenge for having turned these once perky tits into the monstrous mammaries that now lay before us.

Another day in paradise.

We would eat in silence hoping beyond hope that we could finish our cereal and get out the door before some battle would erupt and further spoil an already spoiled day. No such luck. "There are ants in my puffed wheat" I said. "No there's not" my Mom would assert 'That's bran" 'This bran is doing the backstroke" I said. "You kids don't appreciate anything I do around here... I don't know why I even bother... I try so hard to get up and give you a good breakfast and get you off to school.

I often wondered if you could open up her head and peer

inside if it would look like the game board of snakes and ladders.

Another one of her favorite meals was navy beans. This meal requires a little bit of prep time but the results are well worth it. Not beans slow baked in a molasses and brown sugar sauce but boiled white, naked beans. It's quite a sophisticated recipe.

Get a fairly big tub, perhaps an old galvanized washing tub. Rinsing it out is optional. Place it on the stove and place a family size bag of white navy beans in the bottom. Twenty pounds should do the trick. Cover the beans with water. Turn the burner on high and bring the beans to a boil. Put a chunk of some nondescript beef in with the beans. Ask your local butcher to empty his gut bucket if you're having trouble choosing your cut of meat. If you do not have beef feel free to substitute with walrus grizzle. Continue to boil for a few days or until the meat is tender to the fork and easily pulls apart. Now slop this mess on to some plates and watch everyone dig in. Be sure to have plenty of ketchup on hand for those who prefer to spice things up.

On top of the refrigerator was a wooden bowl. Experiments involving fruit flys were constantly being carried out in this vessel. We use to try and guess what kind of fruit was in the bowl? It was particularly challenging when the fruit turned a grayish greenish color and grew fur. At some time in their incubation period the fruit would begin to morph into different shapes.

It wasn't that she couldn't cook, it was that she was just so damned lazy she wouldn't cook. But, when the spotlight was on her she could dress out a table with the best of them.

My Father would invite his top customers to the house for drinks and hors d'oevre around Christmas time. He would use this occasion to reward his customers and to showcase his products. Mom would put the whole thing together. And why not? She would be hob knobbing with the best chefs in the city. The finest culinary minds in the surrounding area would gather around her table and sample some seafood delights prepared for and presented by Olivia, City Fish's' own Executive Chef.

She would begin a couple of days early by boiling up pounds

20

of prawns. When you're cooking prawns by the twenty pound box you have to start early in order to get the smell out of your house. Prawns have a heavy, musty smell when you boil a lot of them. It would be minus ten below zero outside but she would have the back door wide open to combat the condensation and the smell. The neighborhood cats would gather all along the top rail of the picket fence in the backyard driven to distraction by the smells coming out of Mom's kitchen. Next on the list for preparation was lobster. A City Fish pickup truck would arrive with a case of live lobster the day before the event. That night Dad would bring home one of the knives from the store. The broiler was turned on and the rack moved up in the oven. Dad would take a lobster from the case and turn it on its back while holding it in his hand. With one swipe of the knife he would cut the lobster in half run it under the tap and place it under the broiler. The lobster or more correctly, half the lobster would still be moving. This procedure was repeated until the case was empty and there were forty eight beautiful red backed lobster halves.

All this seafood was put on ice in the basement. In pails and tubs and anywhere there was a receptacle suitable for holding ice. There was an old fridge that was used for holding beer that was reenlisted as a cold storage facility. The refrigerator in the kitchen was emptied, thank god, and filled with prawns and lobster. The day of the event was dedicated to decorating and preparing the vessels for the seafood delicacies. Dad would come home early, the only day of the year he allowed himself to leave the fish store before closing, only to arrive and begin to shuck oysters by the dozen. Mom would be laying out plate after plate in the dining room for her discriminating guests to dig in to a seafood fest unavailable anywhere.

When all preparations were complete and the first guest had not arrived yet she would stand back and admire her masterpiece. There was a punch bowl with a base of ice and on that frozen bed were plump pink prawns piled high. The glasses that hung on the edge of the bowl had a nest of lettuce and her special cocktail sauce. Small silver forks wrapped in a small white napkin were stacked in little bundles around the table. You just used the bunch bowl spoon and took the prawns from the bowl and put them in your cup, prawns and cocktail sauce. There were lobsters on two large platters arranged in a sun design. The heads were to the center of the plate while the tails where facing out, their curved tails all facing in the same direction provided a beautiful design. Where Dad had removed the lobster tomalley, Mom had replaced it with cocktail sauce which gave the dish a deep contrasting red color to the white flesh of the lobster. A platter of oysters on the half shell sat on a bed of rock salt which in turn sat on a bed of ice. These oysters were surrounded by a collection of liqueur glasses that had an oyster and a little lemon, worscteshire sauce, and tobassco. Your choice, oysters plain or dressed. Stacks of Alaskan king crab heaped in the center of the table. She would replenish her delicacies as quickly as her guests could devour them.

This was a table for chefs. There were no women at this function because back then there were no women chefs. Mom was the only woman in the room. She was the center of attention. An entire room full of compliments directed to her and her alone. She must have loved it!

BERNIA: AKA, NANNY:

Bernia Duncan, matriarch of the City Fish empire. She looked like Winston Churchill with rouge. She wore so much face powder that when she was angry, which was most of the time she resembled a dust mop being shaken out. She was all roast beef and yorkshire pudding. English to the core, Rule Britannia and God save the King!

She would pinch your face for what she called "being cheeky." Correct you for poor posture. She would point out total strangers who she felt were dressed nicer than you and comment "why don't you try and look better? There's a nicely dressed lad." She despised my Mother and did not let an opportunity go by where a jab or cutting remark could be thrust like a dagger into her heart. And, she would never let my parents forget that she had provided financial assistance for the purchase of the house at 541 Aldous.

My Father respected his Ma and took great pains to live up to her expectations which must have been extremely difficult as one never quite knew where she had placed the bar. After his Father's death I am sure that working alongside of her for many years, seeing her hands in brine all day, hair sprinkled with fish scales and freezing in the winter all day in the store, his heart must have gone out to his mother. I wonder if he had a strong urge to reel in his heart when she announced she was going to marry Percival Winchester.

Percival Winchester worked in the men's clothing shop adjacent to the fish store. If ever there was a match made in heaven this union between Bernia Duncan and Percival Winchester was surely it. He was a year older than Bernia's eldest boy. He was gay. He had infantile penile syndrome. He smoked White Owl cigars and when he had one in his mouth his head resembled a bird house. The cigar providing the perch and his thin lips wrapped around it looked like the bird hole. But he was a nicely dressed lad.

Bernia assigned the moniker to him of "Nunk." He was not to be addressed as a grandfather, or an uncle, he was a Nunk. So their handle for the purposes of the grandchildren was Nanny and Nunk.

Nunk was always trying to take either me or my brother to the YMCA for a swim. I hated the water so I never went. My brother went with him once. Later that night as we lay in our beds he told me that Nunk had jumped him in the shower. I wasn't old enough to understand what a jump was but I knew from the way my brother had told the story that I didn't want to be jumped by Nunk.

Bernia and Percival lived in New Smyrna, Florida. They lived there courtesy of the City Fish and Poultry Company. New Smyrna in the late fifties and early sixties was a beach with a couple of hot dog stands. Bernia and Percival lived back in the glades on a couple of acres of mosquito infested quasi jungle.

One summer I was sent to visit them. The first thing they did with you was take you to Shanty Town to show you how the darkies lived. Run down shacks and beat up white Cadillacs made up the assets of Shanty Town. The segregation movement was not on the march yet and the darkies were segregated to an area of town that was of no use to anyone. My grandmother would tell you all kinds of interesting trivia concerning the darkies. "Did you know that when the little Negro boys get dirty they turn white?" Bernia and Percival weren't even aware that they were red neck assholes.

THE KIDS

My parents were married just at the end of the war and upon my father's honorable discharge from the Royal Canadian Air Force he went to work at the fish store with his Mother and Brother.

Glenn and Olivia moved into a little house on the beach strip and there, hatched the first of their four children.

James was a blonde haired, blue eyed boy. James's creativity would be his claim to fame in future years. A couple of years later Julie joined the cast at the beach house. Julie, the mysterious, secretive, play it close to the vest sister.

By now the little beach house was becoming too small to hold the ensemble. My Mother was pregnant with me so a house, with the monetary assistance of my Father's Mother, was purchased on Aldous Avenue in the east end of Hamilton. Later in my life my Mother never missed an opportunity to remind me of how happy they were in the beach house and that they would never have moved except that they needed more room because of her being pregnant with me. She made me feel as if somehow I was responsible for her being pregnant. I guess it never dawned on her that everything I had to do with it was after the fact. The truth about why they had to move was that the little house on the beach strip was slowly and steadily sinking in the sand. When they originally had moved into the house there were two steps up to the front porch and now there was one step down.

I was born at Saint Joseph's hospital in the morning. My mother said "Saint Joe's was the worst hospital around. All my other kids were born at the Henderson which had a much nicer maternity ward." My fault again.

The last to audition for the Duncan playhouse was Elizabeth. Apparently, a complete surprise to my parents, or so they said. Elizabeth was late for her casting call but when she made her entrance to the center stage she did it with flare. She was born on

Father's Day and was the apple of my Father's eye. My Dad always referred to her as young Elizabeth, overstating the obvious.

Elizabeth's curriculum vita was that Elizabeth was, young Elizabeth.

With the troupe gathered it was time to begin the performance.

541 ALDOUS AVENUE

It was a red brick, two story, single family dwelling in a working class neighborhood that blended in with the other homes on the street. A brick front porch with cement steps leading up parallel to the front provided a larger front porch seating area. Under the living room windows was an angel stone façade. Cedar trees accented the angles of construction and a huge Manitoba Maple tree sat in the center of the front lawn. An asphalt driveway ran between the neighbors and our place, the space being just big enough to squeeze a Pontiac sedan into with little room to open the doors so most of the time the family car sat out in the driveway. In the summer time there were green canvas awnings covering the front porch, the four front windows and the two upstairs bedroom windows, front and back of the house. The house had been built in the forties so all the windows were single pane. In the winter outside storm windows were mounted on the front living room windows. It would be years until our parents realized that it just might be a good idea to get storm windows for the children's upstairs bedroom windows. In the summer all the windows were covered with screen windows. My brother and I would pee out the bedroom window through the screen and laugh hilariously as the little golden stream would scatter into tiny droplets as it passed through the screen.

The back yard was big. Most of the other houses on the block had garages at the end of their driveways which took up a lot of space but we didn't. It was probably the best feature of the house.

In later years my mother insisted on adding on to the back of the house what she called a sun porch. A monstrous wooden affair that nobody ever used because it was not heated so it couldn't be used in the winter time. In the summer time no one wanted to sit inside. After the first year the only one who used the sun porch was the cat. A big black male who would piss in the corners and piss on the moldy old couch marking his territory and adding his horrible presence to the already questionable ambiance of the sun porch. Mom fixed the cat. I mean she really fixed him. The cat would come home from a night of carousing, bloodied and torn up. He would crawl up on the back of the moldy couch and bleed all over it. The cat saw the sun porch as his personal recovery room. She made my brother take him to the vets and have him neutered. My brother put up a pretty good defense on behalf of the cat but eventually lost the argument. Figaro would still go out at night. He probably just sat on side lines wondering what all the excitement was about.

For lawn maintenance we had an almost impossible to push hand mower. My Father decided that on Sundays I should be responsible for cutting and raking the backyard. It was of no consequence that the hand mower weighed more than I did. Just because the handles to push this behemoth were above my head was no reason to shrink from my responsibility. Rowers on Roman galley ships had an easier task. At least they had the opportunity of a quick death. And then there was the raking of the grass clippings. Now this all took place on Sunday. The day that the Seagrams flowed like water, the day when my Father would take the kitchen table up for a spin. Well I guess to add to his warped fantasies the back yard would become his private parade square. Somewhere in between fuel ups for the next flight he would stroll out to the grass and run the toe of his foot along the grass. If any clippings flipped up I would have to rake the entire yard again. Now you don't have to be a statistician to figure out how many times you can get grass clippings to jump in a grassed yard.

But the real adventures took place on the inside of the house. What took place on the inside made the cat's pissing on Mom's sun porch look positively cultured.

The children were garrisoned on the second floor. Originally there were pressed cardboard walls and rough board flooring. The addition of gyproc walls and hardwood flooring helped aesthetically but without insulation in the walls and ceiling the upstairs remained little more than cold storage in the winter. The wooden sash windows would swell and split at the seams when the ice formed and allowed the wind to spill through. On the cold days you could see your breath.

In the summer it was an oven. The only ventilation came from the small front window. A screened frame was inserted to keep the mosquitoes on the outside but there was always the uncontrollable urge to insert a pencil point into and between the little wire squares. If you gently put pressure on the pencil the little square would become a little circle, just big enough for a mosquito to get through. No matter how many times they would replace the screens the little mosquito port holes would appear.

To access the upstairs you ascended a flight of steep wooden stairs off the living room. This staircase acted like a moat to protect us from our parents. Mom being the agile athlete that she was, was not about to haul three hundred pounds up a flight of stairs for just any reason. As it turned out she decided that there were few reasons to climb those stairs. She rarely visited the second floor unless of course it was to act out some ludicrous fantasy that she didn't know what was happening up there. Once or twice a year she would huff and puff her way to the top of the stairs where she would yell "look at this place, it's a pig sty, how can you live like this, there are the clothes I just ironed laying on the floor, it smells like dirty socks, it smells like pee." Thanks for visiting Mom.

First of all, she knew exactly what was happening, she simply chose to ignore it. Secondly, we did look at the place; we simply chose to ignore it. Third, a pig sty was cleaner, if the SPCA had happened on livestock being cared for in the manner our mother took care of her children, they would have had her arrested. Fourth, we didn't know any other way to live. Fifth, there were never any clothes that she had just ironed laying on the floor, there were clothes on the floor but she had never ironed anything. Sixth, of course it smelled like dirty socks, my brother and I wore our socks until they were so hard we couldn't get them on our feet. Seventh, all of us were bed wetter's. The best part about winter on the second floor was that unlike the summer months your eyes didn't sustain urine burns from the fumes that accumulated and had nowhere to exhaust. She would have had to be living on another planet not to have known what was going on at the top of the stairs.

The extent of her exertion put forward to understand what her children were about in the upper chambers was when she would hear some loud crash hit the floor, be it a lamp, one of our socks, some furniture or a kid. She would stand at the bottom of the steps and yell, "what was that," where upon a chorus of kids in perfect synchronization would yell back down, "nothing". And where was Dad when all this was going on? Living on another planet.

Supper was at 6:30 every evening when the family would gather at the kitchen table, (during the week it was grounded). Most other families ate around four or five because their fathers worked at the Steel Company or Defasco. Our Dad didn't close the fish store until 6:00 PM. He would come through the back door, through the kitchen, into my parent's bedroom and remove his fishy smelling sweaters and assume his position at the head of the table. The seating arrangement was always the same. Moving clockwise, beginning with my Father at the head of the table, Mom, Elizabeth on my Fathers right, James at the opposite end, Julie, and me within an easy reach of my Dad's grasp. This positioning was necessary for my Father to be able to cuff me on the back of the head or haul me out of my chair for a full blown ass spanking depending on the severity of what I had said or didn't say or done or not done. And there were so many opportunities for these offenses to have taken place. School, home, somewhere in the neighborhood and right here at the kitchen table. The fact is that if there was a place in the universe you didn't want to be at 6:30 PM weekdays, it was on the left side of the kitchen table, next to my Dad at 541 Aldous.

* * *

Many homes have a laundry chute. A central location that you can drop dirty clothes and linens through to a receptacle, usually a laundry basket, near the washing machine and the dryer. This is a great idea. It saves steps and keeps the laundry in a tidy bundle waiting to be cleaned. We had a similar set up, except it was a little less tidy.

On the main floor of the house was a short hallway connecting the bathroom, kitchen, master bedroom, living room and dining room. At the end of this axis hallway was the door to the cellar steps. The cellar was a world unto its own. It was not a finished basement like most homes had. A place where the family watched TV together and perhaps played pool or entertained their friends. No, our basement was a dingy, dark, and musty place. Filled with cobwebs and a permanent layer of dust that was so thick you could smell it. In the center of the basement was an old gravity oil furnace. It had once been fired by coal but had been converted to oil at some later time. There were several walls that had been constructed by someone who had made a weak attempt at turning the basement into usable space. They had failed miserably. And I was thankful for that. It was a great place for a kid to imagine that he was in the inner sanctum of Zorro's cave. It was easy to pretend that you were a fireman in the bottom of the Titanic. It was not hard to make believe that you were deep down in a mine shaft prospecting for gold. The only interruption to the endless fantasies was when the cellar door would open and somebody would throw a shirt, skirt, bed sheet, underwear or peed in pajamas down the cellar steps on to a wooden landing of sorts at the bottom of the steps. That was our laundry chute. Simply open the door to the basement and heave away any and all dirty clothing where it will lie on the floor until Mom gets around to doing the washing.

On the back wall of the basement, under a small window that

looked out onto the driveway at eye level with the ants were two laundry tubs. The laundry tubs were made from a ferrous material. They were huge, square tanks. Each sink would have been capable of floating a small commercial trawler. A white wringer washer stood in front of the tubs. Hoses were attached to the taps over the tubs and were the source of water for the machine. In the bottom of the washing machine was a plug that you could unscrew and drain the dirty water from the washing machine. The water ran out onto the cement floor and drained into an indented floor drain. Like many other phenomena exclusive to our house alone, I had never seen this kind of set up in any of my friend's houses or at any relative's house. The closest arrangement for washing clothes this way would have been beating your clothes on a rock by a river.

After the stack of clothes at the bottom of the cellar steps got so high that the view from the top of the stairs gave the impression that if you stepped of the top step you would be drowned in a sea of dirty socks and soiled bed sheets, Mom would do the laundry. She would drag the dirty items over to her machine. The agitator would swish the dirt out of the clothes and then she would run all the items through the wringer into a laundry tub that was full of clean rinse water and then through the wringer again and into the adjacent tub. The wringer was the tricky part. This was the part of the machine that could claim a life. Here was a mechanical gadget that had more horror stories attached to it than Hollywood had movies. The wringers could catch your hand and drag your whole arm through until all the skin had been ripped clean off. If it got you by the hair it would pull all your hair out and take your scalp too. With a machine this dangerous lurking in the basement it is no wonder she did the laundry only when you had been wearing your last pair of underwear until you were not wearing your last pair of underwear.

Finally my Mom convinced my Dad to buy her an electric clothes dryer. When the dryer guys came they discovered that the house wasn't wired to take a dryer. So the electrician came and discovered that the paper cartridges weren't up to code and that a new electrical box would have to be fitted before he could wire the dryer. A thousand dollars later mom had her new dryer and my brother and I had something new to play with.

"I'll betch'a it would be fun for you to spin around in there," James said.

"I'm afraid it would cook me." I replied.

"Look, there's a temperature dial. We can set it on cool and then you won't get burnt. You get in there and I'll give you a ride."

So I went for a ride in the new Sears dryer. The next week the Sears repairman came and replaced the drive belt. He wanted to know what kinds of loads mom had been putting in her dryer. She told the repair guy that she had only used the dryer once.

"Have you kids been using the dryer? Whats been going on with my new dryer?"

"Nothing."

* * *

Somewhere and at sometime our Mother must have read in one of the leading medical journals such as Reader Digest that exposing your boys to some form of organized gymnastics would help them to develop into productive, contributing citizens. Or, she just wanted to get rid of us for a few hours on Saturday morning. Whatever the reason, we found ourselves as members of the Mr. Tribble's Tumbling Troop. We would meet in the local high school gym where Mr. Tribble would teach the rudimentary skill sets necessary to achieve Olympic status tumbling tricks or just enough to join a circus.

Mr. Tribble was a compact kind of guy. He looked like some kind of athletic kit that you could purchase at Canadian Tire. Sort of an in home gym instructor. He wore navy blue sweatpants and a pair of sparkling white sneakers, a white muscle shirt and a whistle on a white rope hung around his neck completing the ensemble. He was fond of grabbing me by the arm and holding it straight up until I was near tangling in the air looking like some scared squirrel that had been caught in a trap. All the time he would be yelling at the class, "See how skinny this little arm is? If this skinny little arm can do hand springs why can't you big fellows do one?" Then he would drop me and like a squirrel that had worked itself free from a trap, I would scurry back to my position in line with the others.

We would use the wooden horses and the spring boards for our routines and sometimes we would team up to perform certain types of tumbling routines. My brother and I would invariably team up together. I had a lot of confidence in my brother so we could perform some pretty good stunts. My favorite teamed trick was; my brother would lie on his back with his knees brought up and his feet on the floor. I would run toward him and use his knees as a tumbling horse throwing my body into a somersault while he would push on my back so that I could gain height and after a complete revolution I would land on my feet. We practiced this all the time. We got so we could achieve a lot of height and a great distance. The faster I ran and the harder he pushed the higher and further I would go. We could see ourselves on the Ed Sullivan Show. Right before Topo Gigio came out Ed would introduce our act, "Right here, on this stage, just before we bring out the little Italian mouse Topo Gigio, for your tumbling entertainment, a couple of youngsters from Canada. John and James. Let's have a big hand for John and James."

If we were going to appear on the Ed Sullivan Show we would have to practice every chance we got. One of those chances we got was in the living room. Mom had gone out shopping. We had the living room to ourselves. We pushed as much of the furniture to the side as we could and moved the big, round, oak coffee table as close to the end of the room as possible. James got down on his back with his knees up. I stood facing him. I gave a little jump, a movement I had been practicing to make me look light on my feet. I began my approach towards my brother. I placed my hands on his knees and began my somersault. His hands were on my back pushing me up. I was half way around in my somersault when I came down with my back hitting the big, round, oak coffee table. The room wasn't as big as we had thought. When I came down onto the top of the table, as luck would have it, I came down with the grain of the wood in perfect alignment with my spine. The table split right down the center as straight as a die.

This was no ordinary coffee table. It was solid oak. It had once been a dining table and the pedestal had been cut down to the appropriate height. Because it was Dad who cut the pedestal to size, Mom had embellished the story that Dad had built the table. Although I had never seen my Father with a tool of any kind in his hand, I believed her. Now, with Dad's masterpiece lying in ruins and Mom on no set ETA to home we had to act fast regardless of what course we chose.

James said we could fix the table. This was certainly new territory for us. We broke things! We took apart clocks, watches, toys, and the little diver in our aquarium and window screens. "How are we gonna do that, James?"

"We can nail it back together at the base and no one will ever know the difference."

Off we went to the basement to find some nails and a hammer. The only nails in the house were one inch finishing nails. Tiny nails used for fine work like installing new screens in windows. They were more like tacks than nails. We grabbed a handful and a hammer and headed back up stairs.

The sight of the coffee table was sickening. It made a huge wooden V and lay on the floor like some giant turtle that had been hit by lightening in the center of its back. We positioned the table in its normal place, we didn't think moving this behemoth around after we had repaired it would be necessary. "But what about when Mom vacuums? Don't you think she'll notice?" I asked,

"Don't be stupid, we'll probably have graduated and moved

out by the time she moves this thing to vacuum." My brother had a point.

We managed to put thirty seven finishing nails into the base of the coffee table. It still wasn't holding. In fact the weight of a small ash tray would have caused it to collapse. We were running out of time. "Put all the furniture back, and whatever stuff was on the coffee table," said James. "We'll fix it when we have more time, until then, keep your mouth shut. Listen to me John, when Mom gets home don't look at the table. Just act normal. Okay?"

"Yeah, okay."

I'm kneeling on one of the chairs by the front window when a taxi pulls up in front of the house. Mom spills out of the back seat onto the sidewalk while the cab driver gets her grocery bags out of the trunk and they make their way to the front door. "Get away from the window. Do you want to blow it?" My brother has years of experience on me and is a lot better at deception than I am. I swing my legs around and assume a devil may care pose. Except for my beet red head and my uncontrollable farting, I think I have my act together. The farting she won't notice, the beet red head could be a problem. Mom comes and takes one look at me and says," What's wrong with you?"

"Nothing."

"James? What's wrong with your brother?"

"Nothing."

I get out of my chair and start across the room acting quite indignant that our Mother does not take our word at face value. I gave a little jump, a movement I had been practicing to make me look light on my feet. I tripped and fell forward, my chin hit the table on the way down. The table split in two. My brother yelled, "Look what he did!"

We might have pulled it off. Mom does a perfunctory physical inspection of me to assure herself that my neck isn't broken. Enough of a check that an inquest would absolve her of any criminal negligence then begins a thorough examination of the coffee table. She discovers that the pedestal of the table resembles a porcupine. Thirty seven finishing nails, their points exposed and searching in vain for something to grasp. James doesn't miss a beat, "I guess Dad isn't the carpenter you thought he was, eh?"

"Wait till your Father gets home."

We did wait for our Father to get home. We waited in sheer terror. The way Mom had carried on about the table and the fact that, "Your Father made that table with his own two hands," like he was going to make it with somebody else's hands. I figure we were probably going to die. My thinking was that if he can beat me for doing menial stuff, what is he going to do if it's important like breaking a table that he made with his own two hands?

As soon as my Dad walks in the door my Mother waltz's him into the living room where the great oak coffee table still lay on the floor in its two halves. "How'd that happen?" he says off offhandedly "The boys were tumbling in the living room."

"Why the sam hill didn't you stop them?" James and I are standing off to the side and we can't believe what we are hearing. This is just too good to be true. It looks like it will be Moms fault. "I was out at the store. They did this when I was gone!"

"Well what do you want me to do about it?"

"Don't you think they deserve to be punished?" We thought that was a foul. If Dad couldn't think up a reason to hit us then she shouldn't be allowed to suggest it.

"Okay, you guys carry that table out to the garbage."

And that was it. Lying in our beds that night we figured that Dad probably hated the table and was sick of Mom telling the story of how he had made it with his own two hands. Being the honest guy he was he was probably glad the table was gone.

ELIZABETH

The big turquoise Pontiac Strato Chief swung into the driveway. My sister and brother were there to greet the newest arrival to the family. My Father went around to the passenger's side and helped Mother out of the car. In her arms was a bundle of new baby sister.

I was just barely old enough to somewhat understand the significance of this event. There was a person and that person was somehow connected to our lives and would be forever. I do not remember my Mother being pregnant. Physically she probably didn't look any different and so did not prompt any questions. But I do not remember any of those poignant learning moments where the mother puts her son's hand or head on her tummy and says "that's your new baby sister or brother. He or she is soon coming out of my tummy to meet you." There was one day when Elizabeth was laying on the bed in a diaper and her shriveled umbilical cord was exposed. It looked like a dried white larvae. I was afraid for Elizabeth and called out to Mom, "what's coming out of Elizabeth's belly button?" My Mom said "that was how Elizabeth ate while she was attached to Mommy." I didn't ask any more questions, that was enough. There is only so much biological information a five year old can absorb in one day.

Once, it was a Sunday, perhaps my parents were participating in a kitchen table fly in, my sister Julie and I took Elizabeth for a ride in her stroller. We walked down a block, around the corner to the left and up two blocks, left and back down the street. As we were crossing the last street we lifted the front wheels of the stroller in order to overcome the curb and the back rest of the stroller opened and out slid Elizabeth head first onto the pavement. Her head went clunk. In the blink of an eye, we slid her back the way she had come out of the stroller, closed and locked the back rest into position. Elizabeth never made a sound. Never made a peep. Did not change the expression on her face. Julie was adamant, "when we get home you don't say anything." This was a precursor to the famous "nothing" philosophy. Obviously I was coming of age and beginning my training in the "they don't need to know, want to know, keep them in the dark" school.

So when we got home we had been nowhere, we had seen no one and we had done nothing,

SCHOOL AND PUNISHMENT

I think you always anticipate your first day of school as an experience to look forward to. Especially if you have older siblings attending school. Makes you kind of feel that your one of the big kids now. I know I was looking forward to my first day. I knew it would be a day to remember for the rest of my life. My education, edification and enlightenment would be colored and shaped by the events of this momentous day.

Saint John's was a parochial school attached to the Saint John the Baptist parish. Roman Catholics needed to educate their children separately from the general public. We had secrets that were not to be shared with those who were not of the RC faith because they weren't going to heaven anyway.

We were taught that if they hadn't been baptized they did not qualify for heaven. This dogma caused a serious problem for our family. Dad wasn't a catholic. Dad not being a catholic caused us other problems too. For example; Catholics always had more holidays than the public school system and it was just natural for a kid to flaunt this perk by passing by a public school during recess and letting them know that it was "all saints day" so we could stay at home and eat all the Halloween candy we had gathered the night before. Which would elicit the standard response, "ah, you're a dirty catholic" and the standard retort was, "ah, you're a dirty protestant and you're not going to heaven." Having a Father who was a protestant posed certain questions as to his prospects for an afterlife and whether he was a dirty protestant or not. Mostly we just refrained from and simply observed our peers as they did unto their fellow man. I always thought that it was terribly unfair to condemn all those people, especially all the babies who never did anything to anybody, to eternal damnation. But, the church had an answer for that dilemma. If, for example, a baby had not done anything wrong they would go to Limbo. This was a place similar to heaven except you didn't get to see God. Then there was purgatory.

This was a place for a person who did stuff that was bad, but not really, really bad. They would go to purgatory and were burnt for a while but eventually you got to go to heaven and see our benevolent God.

Being that Saint John's was a catholic school most of the teachers were Nuns. These were women that were all married to Jesus. If Jesus thought he had it rough while he was here on earth, he must have been pissed when he found out that he would be married to some of the meanest old hags ever. I always thought that their black and white stiffly starched habits must have been intolerably uncomfortable because they were always in a bad mood.

Nuns were also martial arts experts. Specialists in the art of JODO, stick fighting. They could wield a pointer or a yard stick to their will. And so to the victim under it. After only one year of instruction from a Nun your hands and knuckles would look as if you were a veteran professional football lineman. Beating a student about the head and hands with a wooden dowel was an example of the Separate School system at its finest.

The school crest displayed a student with a yard stick and a pointer crossed over his head and the motto, "never too soon."

So it's my first day of school and I have been told to go the principal's office, Sister Joanie-Marie. She is standing in front of me with this giant starched head piece that gives her the look of a huge black and white cobra that is about to strike. "What were you doing on the grass in front of the school?"

"Nothing."

"Did you not know that you should never step on the grass in front of the school?"

"No."

"Every student knows not to step on the grass in front of the school. Why don't you?"

"Cause it's my first day"

"Well, you must have read the KEEP OFF THE GRASS sign?"

"I can't read. I came to school to learn to read."

"Well I think we should give you something to help you remember to keep off the grass. Hold out your hands." Thinking that I may be about to receive some magical talisman blessed by the Pope and able to produce incredible memory faculties I thrust out my hands eagerly for the prize I was about to receive. Sister Joanie Marie produced a two and half inch by fourteen inch leather strap which she immediately began beating my hands with. And Sister Joanie-Marie was no slouch; this was not her first rodeo. She gripped the leather strap firmly with her right hand and with her left hand she cupped the elbow of her right arm for support. With wide arcing strokes she applied her trade with much vigor.

In a previous life Sister Joanie Marie was likely a boson aboard some sailing vessel which had a reputation for strict discipline and was renowned for her application of the cat a nine tails.

Who made this corporal device? This leather strap was made for the specific intention of beating little kids. Was there a catalog called S & M for children? Was it in the Grand and Toy school supplies section indexed under abuse? When it came time for ordering the years school supplies did the Nuns sit around making suggestions such as, "We will need one hundred and thirty wooden pointers, one hundred and fifty yard sticks, a dozen leather straps, oh, we had better make that two dozen leather straps, we certainly don't want to run out of straps like we did last year. And some chalk."

I went to school for another twelve years but that was the last day I ever attended.

* * *

When it came to beating children my Dad's weapon of choice was the bean bat. We kids named it that perhaps to bring some levity to a subject that truly struck terror into hearts. To hear the dreaded command, "get the bean bat" meant that you wouldn't be sitting down for a while.

My mother was into the latest child rearing tomes of the fifties. Doctor Spock and various articles from the Reader's Digest gave her all the necessary tools she felt she needed for bringing up her children. Along the way some expert had suggested that if you hit your child with your bare hand the child would associate the pain with the parent, however, if you hit the child with some other object, then the child would associate the object with the pain therefore avoiding any psychological damage betwixt the child and the parent...what fucking crap. I don't know if the article included a suggested list of items to clobber your kid with but I'm damn sure the bean bat was not on the list.

The bean bat was a hard rubber badminton raguet leftover long after the shuttlecocks and netting had been lost or destroyed. When you swung this racquet onto a kid's ass the flexible shaft would whip the head at near the speed of light coming to a violent and abrupt halt against the buttocks flesh of an eight year old. Thank you Doctor Spock for that incredible insight and allowing us to grow up with our bums resembling the perfect waffle.

NOTHING

The boy's bedroom was kind of a Norman Rockwell does acid motif. My mother had spared no expense when it came to replicating the set of Wally and the Beaver's bedroom. The only problem was that Wally and the Beaver didn't live in this bedroom, James and John did. Against the two far walls were two rock maple beds. One on each side of the window. The bedspreads were brown with roped off squares containing pictures of ships hardware. Under the window was a bedside table with a rock maple lamp standing on three legs. The lamp stand had a replica of a little ships wheel and was crowned with a cardboard lamp shade depicting a square rigged vessel under full sail.

Above each of the rock maple headboards were matching wall lamps, with little ships wheels and matching cardboard lamp shades with the same ships as the one on the bedside table.

When you entered the room, on the right, running along the wall there was a double wide rock maple dresser of six drawers, three for James to keep his clothes neatly folded in and three for John to keep his clothes neatly folded in. On top of the dresser was a ten gallon aquarium with guppies, neon tetras and zebra fish. Bubbles were expelled from the helmet of a little deep sea diver standing on the sandy bottom and waving to all who peered in to the underwater scene. To the left side of the room was a large rock maple wardrobe for the brothers to share. In this large cabinet we would hang our Sunday suits and our dress shirts.

The ornamentation of the sailing ships was lovely, however, the ships theme would have been more appropriate for my brother and I had she purchased a cargo container.

This picture perfect bedroom designed by Lord Baden Powell suitable for Mickey Rooney and the Hardy Boys would last about as long as it would take to get to the first item, the little ships wheel on the bedside table lamp. It was held on by a single brass nail. It took no time at all to pry that off.

The cardboard lampshades with the pictures of ships under full sail were dismasted and smashed upon the rocks in short order. Soon only a wire frame sat like a drunken halo above a sixty watt bulb. The bedspreads found a new home under the bed. The wall lamps met the same fate as their bedside table cousin. The neatly folded clothes in the dresser eventually came to live with the bedspread under the beds. The aquarium became a laboratory dedicated to experiments in evolution. If you didn't add water or feed the fish they would have to grow legs and be forced to leave the aquarium in search of sustenance, or so our hypothesis ran. After a time the water level became so low the little diver just sort of began to fart out of the top of his helmet. No need to leave your Sunday clothes hanging in the wardrobe. Not when it was only Tuesday. Especially not when you could hide in the wardrobe and scare the shit out of your big brother when he came into the room... He retaliated immediately. By stuffing me into the wardrobe and pushing it over onto its front, imprisoning me by the weight of the wardrobe and me inside. It hit the floor with a resounding crash. Mom was at the bottom of steps yelling, "What was that?" Julie from her bedroom yelled back "nothing", James standing on the backside of the now coffin like structure yelled back "nothing" and me from inside my new crypt yelled back "nothing." My voice sounded like it was coming from underground, muffled and hollow. She wasn't buying it this time. She started up the stairs. There was no time to lose. In order to keep her from entering our room we would have to greet her at the top of the steps looking as sweet and innocent as the Von Trapp Family before she got more than half way up the stairs.

Then, when she could eyeball her progeny she would realize the futility of her quest and let gravity assist returning her bulk to the main floor.

One good kick and the press board back of the wardrobe came flying off. Houdini had done it and we arrived with our Cheshire grins, in record time, at the top of the stairs. "What was that?" she squeaked, out of breath and turning a deep shade of red. In perfect unison we replied, "Nothing."

THE MOUNTAIN PEOPLE

The Niagara Escarpment, a giant ridge of rock running from the Niagara River to the top of the Bruce Peninsula. It is a geological formation some four hundred and fifty million years old. As the back stop to the City of Hamilton it rises some five hundred feet, pretty well straight up. For the kids who braved its wilds, it was the greatest unsupervised playground in the world.

Most Hamiltonians referred to the escarpment as Hamilton Mountain. Of course most Hamiltonians had not been been further west than Brantford so what would they know what a mountain looked like. Back in the fifties, butting against the escarpment the city literally ended there. I few houses crested the mountain brow, but that was about it.

It was a green dark forest of haunting beauty. Creatures of amazing abundance darted, hopped and skittered through this mystical landscape. Salamanders, toads and garter snakes by the score called this place home. It was the perfect stage for Act I of what was to become the most terrifying experience of my entire life.

I guess I was six or seven at the time. My brother had hauled me up the mountain on an afternoon's excursion. We had started a fire and began to warm the can of Heinz beans we had stolen from the kitchen cupboard. We used tree bark fashioned into crude spoons. "Ya' know John, these woods are full of awful people who force boys like us to do all kinds of horrible things."

"Like what?"

"Just really bad stuff. No one has ever lived to tell about it after they've received the letter."

"What letter?"

"The letter that tells them where they have to go and meet them or they'll kill everybody in their family."

"Can we go home now?"

"Sure" said James. I was scared shitless but I figured it was him just trying to scare me because he never said anything about the letter again.

I opened my eyes and the fluids leaked out of my body. My chest sank, the blood stopped circulating. My head flushed red hot. My body froze in the prone position on the bed. I began to cry. I tried to call out but I could only make whimpering sounds. My brother was awake and asked, "What is it? What's the matter?"

"The letter is here." There, floating above my head was the letter. "Take it down, what's it say?" "James asked," I was blubbering, I could hardly speak. "I can't move."

"Just reach up and get it."

"I can't move." He got out of bed and came over to my bed and lifted my arms to the floating horror dangling just a foot above my head. He placed my hands on the letter and said, "Now pull!" With that the letter detached from what was keeping it in suspension. I held the envelope in my hands. The entire weight of the world was contained in that letter. James wanted me to open the letter but I was having nothing to do with it. I knew what was in the letter. He took it from me and began to open it. I just sat there and whimpered. Making up excuses, "maybe it's come to the wrong place."

"Well I don't think so; it's got your name and my name on the envelope." He was right, there was no mistake. "Besides I don't think the mailman delivered this," he said. James took the letter out of its jacket and unfolded the letter. It was written in red. "Wow! It's written in blood." "It's from the mountain people." He had a scared look on his face as he told me that they wanted us both to come up the mountain to where we had eaten the beans. We were to come this afternoon. We were both to come.

I just began to cry and through great blubbering gulps of air I told James that there was no way I was going up the mountain. He said that he was going.

"But they'll kill you" I cried. "They'll kill us all if I don't."

I stayed in our bedroom all morning. He would stick his head in every now and then to check on me. Finally he came up and announced that he was leaving. He was going up the mountain to see those people. I was as scared and as forlorn as a person could be. I knew I would never see my brother again. I hung around my room until I just couldn't stand it any longer. I had to tell someone what had happened and what was happening. I decided to tell my mother.

I went downstairs and sort of followed her around trying to screw up the courage to tell her that her first born son was probably dead.

I just blurted it out, "They're gonna kill James!" My Mom looked at me with total confusion, "The shoe salesman is going to kill James?" she asked."No, no, his gone up the mountain, the mountain people."

"Well he had better not have gone up the mountain. He's gone to get a new pair of shoes for school. He's known about this all week so he had better not be out goofing off or I'll kill him."

It truly was a masterful tale. He had planted the seed. Let it germinate over a period of several days. He had created circumstances with which to carry out all the necessary actions. He had built the set and all the props. And he knew his audience. I have never, ever been so scared in my life since that morning when the letter, which was suspended by a thread, was hanging over my head.

STUTTER STEPS

Julie was a ballerina. She studied for many years with a well respected studio and developed her talent to a level that gave her a tryout with National Ballet. It was a bitter cold morning when the family was packed into the Pontiac in the wee hours of the morning. We were heading off to The National School of Ballet in Toronto. Julie was auditioning for acceptance to the school. She was quiet, which was not unusual for Julie. More quiet than normal, probably running through her steps and routines that she would be performing for their Board later that morning.

Julie had achieved a level of competence in strong classical ballet techniques. She was quite capable of standing on her toes for as long as she wanted. Those "toe" shoes had blocks of wood that conformed to the shape of the ballet slipper while not necessarily conforming to the shape of the toe that was carrying the entire body weight. Not only standing but jumping from one foot to the other, spinning and generally prancing about. This would be difficult enough on its own but the trick was to make it look like you were not exerting any more energy than a pond spider. She was amazing and I truly admired her talent.

When she got to around sixteen years of age her friends told her that if she continued with her ballet her legs would become fat and ugly. These were her peers that could not even conceive of the discipline required to achieve the level of competence that my sister had reached. These buddies of hers could not begin to understand the sacrifices both physically and mentally that Julie would have endured with the practicing of her craft.

These were friends who didn't have what she had so they had decided she wouldn't have it either.

I think I was more disappointed than anyone else. I was proud of my sisters dancing. I could not understand why my Mother had not put up a bigger stink and had allowed Julie to quit her dance class without much fuss.

Some years later the subject came up between my Mom and I and I pressed her as to why she had not put up a strong and compelling argument for keeping Julie in her dance class. Mom's eyes welled up and she began to unload a burden that she had been carrying around for a long time.

"Julie stuttered when she young."

"Well, okay, lots of kids stutter and grow out of it, obviously she did." answering like it was no big deal. Mom's eyes pleaded for understanding and patience so I settled back for what could be a long and boring story. Something she was quiet accomplished at especially if she was visiting with the Seagrams.

"When we lived on the beach strip Julie spent all her time with Norma who lived across the street." Norma was an adult friend of Julie's, who before her early death from cancer still took Julie for occasional weekend outings even after we had moved to Aldous. All I knew was that they were close. "I mean she spent all her time with Norma" emphasizing the all her time words. "Yeah, so?" Then the tears began to flow. "So when we moved to the house on Aldous she began to stutter and, and." Some bombshell was about to go off. "And she didn't seem to know that I was her mother." "Julie never called me Mom or anything for that matter. She just pined away for Norma and seemed to withdraw into herself. The stuttering got worse until it got to the point she didn't talk to anyone." I continued to let her go away on the weekends to Norma's because I didn't know what else to do. When she would come home I would ask Norma how things had gone and she would say that she and Julie had had grand chats. I was devastated. Julie would talk to Norma but she wouldn't talk to me." This was one hell of a story! I never knew Julie to ever stutter but then again I would have been four or five at most while this was going on. "What's this got to do with her ballet?" I was missing some key information to try and tie this tale together. "I read somewhere that if you have a child that stutters the coordination skills of dancing can help stop the stuttering."

"Really," I said, mostly because I didn't know what else to say. There were a dozen different things whipping through my mind all at the same time. What was my mother doing all day if she wasn't taking care of her kids? Didn't her husband want to know where his daughter was? Didn't she want to know what her daughter was doing, how she was doing, where she was doing it?

Mom always wanted to hang out with what she interpreted as the artsy or the personality types. Whenever it was possible to be seen or to entertain, to be included and associated with these folks she was there. At the time there was a radio announcer that lived on the beach strip just up from Mom's house. Mom had often talked about Lowell and the fun they had when they all lived on the beach strip. I do not remember Dad joining in the conversation. Was the reason Julie was ignored at home because Mom was busy up the street with Mr. Radio?

It was a very sad story and I did not press her any of the answers to my questions that evening except one. "So why didn't you put up a bigger fight when Julie said she would quit ballet?" She simply replied, "It didn't matter anymore." I think that pissed me off more than anything. It didn't matter to whom? If that kind of talent could be swept away without any regard to its development...I guess she was right, it didn't matter anymore.

I have often wondered if the true reason that they moved from the beach strip was not because the little house was sinking in to the sand but that it was my Dad's marriage that was going under.

FLEDGED

By the late sixties all we kids are still around, no one has ended up in jail and we have, for the most part, begun to integrate with the rest of the world. Not through lessons learned in our own house, all that crazy shit continued, but rather because we were intelligent primates able to adapt and to ascertain what was acceptable and unacceptable behavior, sort of. We began to shower on a daily basis, although our Mother would yell at us about the cost of hot water. We changed our clothes quite frequently, although our Mother would yell at us about the cost of hot water and the costs associated with the electricity to run the dryer. But we now knew that these simple, yet effective personal hygiene habits would help us get along out there in the world. The world, something which she had not participated in for some time.

James was working in radio in a little northern station. When people asked my Mother about him she would refer to him as a radio personality. I suppose if you take telephone requests from Larry who wants you to play "Never Ending Love" for Becky Sue, that qualifies you as radio personality.

James got his big break into show business while delivering drugs on his bicycle for a local pharmacy. One of his customers, who happened to be the manager of a radio station, took a liking to James and told him if he got his driver's license he could work weekends as an operator. It was the local rock'n roll station. On Saturday's he worked with the DJ who would count down the *Sensational Sixty* and on Sundays he did the ever popular and wildly energetic remote broadcast from the high mass at the Christ the King cathedral. He was still in High School and when he bombed out one year my Dad threatened him with having to quit the radio job until his studies improved. James graduated High School but in the mean time he had been sending out demo tapes to every radio station and fifty watt hen house that existed. He landed an announcer's position with a little station in Huntsville Ontario. When asked who he was taking to the prom he said "I'm leaving, good bye," and he was gone.

With his back to the family he seldom came for visits. When he did come to visit he and my mother would get drunk. She would smother her little radio personality with adoring kisses. James and Dad would do some kind of Freudian macho warrior crap and early the next morning he would be back in his beat up whatever of a car he had at that time and be tooling his way back to show business.

James showed up at the house one weekend and announced that he was going to marry a girl from Burk's Falls. This came as a bit of a shock to my mother. "Are these the same people you told me about when you were here last? The hillbillies?" "Yes." He hadn't totally remembered that conversation due to an overdose of Vat 69. "You told me that you had met a family of wacko's who lived back in the bush, shot their tractors, and where just a bunch of drunks. Now you tell me you're going to marry one of them. What am I to think?" It didn't matter to James what she thought. "I'm going to bring her down to meet you next weekend."

Next weekend we met his future bride. The future would be in about two months. The wedding was held at her family estate, a barn in a field. The locals came on their tractors, some had bought new checkered shirts. Bernia and Percival had come up from Florida. Junior and Cybil brought them up from the city. They were wearing their fur coats and stoles. They promptly locked the fur coats in the trunk. Personally, I didn't think there was much chance of the locals stealing their fur coats. However, I thought their chances of being shot by mistake were pretty fair. The bride and groom exchanged their vows, the people from the city got back in their cars and went home and the locals passed out.

* * *

Julie had met her future first husband. He possessed some pre-Copernican notion that everything in the universe revolved around him, but he provided her with a safe haven away from the nuthouse she was raised in. He came from a normal, loving environment where the husband went to work and came home happy to be with his family. The husband and wife would go out dancing together and come home sober. On Sundays the wife would make a dinner where they would all sit down together and eat edible, fresh and nutritious food. Conversation would center on what everyone was doing and a general concern and respect was issued to everyone. There was a family cottage where the whole family went to enjoy weekends and holidays and the company of each other. Sharing in the love and joy of this family's environment it would not have mattered to Julie if she were dating Frankenstein. Julie spent as much time as possible with her boyfriend; rarely did she make an appearance at Aldous.

Julie and the Mr. Universe were married and moved into a little house just around the block from Aldous Avenue. It surprised me that she would have moved as close to Mom as she did. She must have figured, and rightly so, that a block and half was way too far for her Mother to walk.

They opened an antique store and Julie began an interior decorating service. This was no surprise. When Julie was young she made every effort to transform her room into something, well, something nice. She made it her mission in life to never live as her mother had lived.

Julie's flare for decorating began at an early age. She once wallpapered her bedroom wall and as an attractive accent she added a Kentucky Fried Chicken bucket which she wallpapered and used for her garbage can. Then she wallpapered the lampshade. Then she wall papered the cross where Jesus was hanging on the wall.

* * *

I too had met and fallen in love with the first of my future divorcees.

I had met Becky through a work related event. I was working for the Public Relations and Safety department of an automobile club. The club sponsored a Safety Crossing Guard clinic in association with the local police force. The object of the clinic was to instruct 12 and 13 year old students how to safely assist younger students crossing busy streets in school zones. We would take students from across the various county school areas to a private camp for one week. We would set up mock intersections for the children to learn the proper procedures to aid them with their crossing guard duties. Becky was a volunteer councilor from one of the townships participating in the clinic.

Mostly, after the students had been bedded down, the councilors fooled around with each other. I was the fool and Becky was the around.

Her Father had been blessed with the most effeminate name known to the English language. Ambrose, he went by Amby. He looked like an Amby, his face was elongated to such an extent you would have thought he had won first prize in a taffy pull; as the taffy. He had his hair flattened across an oversized forehead. He wore a mustache that was thin and always looked wet. And because this was the scene that greeted him in the mirror every morning he was always in a bad mood. He was a nasty little bastard.

Becky's mother worked for the township's local police force. She was a receptionist who wanted to be the chief of police, at least she acted that way. She dressed in a quasi military style with short cropped hair and as many dresses she could find that were adorned with epaulets.

The first time I drove up to Becky's to take her out on a date her mother, the wanna be cop, came marching down the driveway with a pad and pencil in her hand. She stood in front of the car and recorded my license plate number. I asked if she would prefer I could leave a credit card as collateral. That was a huge mistake. God had actually put two of the most humorless people on earth together. I guess he figured there was no reason to spoil two families. The harangue began and lasted for ten minutes. I tried to tell them it was just a little joke and was informed in no uncertain terms what was funny and what was not funny. Which I thought was pretty funny.

Our relationship was not built on a solid foundation. I was lonely, she was lonely. I wanted out of my house and she wanted out of her house. We just leaned on each other. Leaning doesn't make for a strong structure.

After we were married we were always out doing something. I would be out at a bar. She would be out at a bar. They just weren't the same bars. The marriage lasted eighteen months.

* * *

Elizabeth was, young Elizabeth. Living oblivious to what the rest of her siblings knew... that this was a horrible place to be. Elizabeth lived in a world where her mother provided little, if no care and her father was mentally incapable of providing any type of succor necessary for a young girls needs. I would protect her however and whenever I could. Mostly, I became her therapist, probably not her best choice of mental health practitioners, but I did know where she was coming from. Come to think of it, regular training in the psychological disciplines would have left you completely unprepared for dealing with this family and their wing nut behavior. I would listen to Elizabeth's concerns and try to draw real world analogies for what she was being exposed to in her world. Assuring her that someday she would be free of this crazy stuff and into a happier, more loving environment.

THE WHITE WHALE

My Father's day began at 5:00 AM, six days a week. He closed the store at 6:00 PM. This work schedule had gone on probably since he was seventeen. The only break in this schedule he would have ever known would have been during the war.

When he returned to the store after the war he would have gone back with new and exciting experiences. He had a new wife and they shared a romantic little cottage together on the beach. Back then it would not have been polluted and the toxic mess it became in later years. They undoubtedly were in love and starry-eyed, enjoying each other's idealistic, dreamy lives.

Their first son was born and surely this would have been a joyous event in their lives. They were living the dreams that they had dreamt during the war, except Glenn was working at the fish store. This was not the glamorous career of an airline pilot they both had planned.

Bernia owned the business and Junior and Glenn were employees of the business. In the early stages of his marriage he could not have cared less about the proud heritage of a fishmonger and the reputation of City Fish and Poultry Ltd in the community. But as time went by, as the responsibilities increased as his Mother dug her claws in deeper and his Brother came to rely upon him more and more and as the love of his life got bigger and bigger, he came to settle his ambitions on less loftier goals.

When the time came to purchase the home on Aldous, Bernia was there to lend a monetary hand. The claws were beginning to close around this son. Just as when an eagle has her prey in the clutches of her talons, Bernia could not let go. She had already managed to subdue her eldest son Junior. Bernia, and the newly married Junior, and his bride Cybil, were all living in the house in Burlington. So here was Junior, with his new wife, living rent free in a lovely house off the Lakeshore, working for his mother and here was Glenn, given strong financial assistance to purchase a home, working for his Mother. This was a no brainer for her sons that the status quo was the way to go.

But Bernia had a little bomb to drop on the boys. Now that they were safely and permanently indebted to her, both financially and psychologically it was time to announce a change in plans. She was going to marry Percival, the gentleman from the men's clothing store.

Now Junior and Glenn would have known about Percival. They would have probably shared a number of jokes at his expense behind his back, but Percival would have the last laugh. Not only was he going to marry their mother, they were going to pay for the wedding and for everything else as long as they lived. Bernia and Percival were going to retire to Florida. Percival was one year older than Junior. Junior and Glenn were going to pay for his retirement and life style, married to their Mother, forever.

The new business agreement would provide for equal shares, thirty three, thirty three and thirty three, one share being retained by the lawyer. It was a standard partnership agreement except for one unusual clause that Bernia had insisted upon being inserted. In effect the clause read that any partner upon being diagnosed with any mental affliction would not be entitled to any benefit and that their shares would be forfeited and distributed to the remaining shareholders on an equal basis.

The boys were to respond with jubilation that they now were partners in City Fish and Poultry Ltd. and would adjust to the part about their Mother and her gigolo driving off south to set up housekeeping in Florida. "Have fun my Laddies and keep those cheques coming!"

So now the boys were in charge. In charge of what? There were still fish to be ordered and paid for, fish to be cleaned, fish to be delivered and paid for. They were both pretty good at the fish to be cleaned part but neither had dealt with the office end of things. You had to pay the suppliers for the fish and you had to collect for the fish you sold. It was obvious help was needed in this area but where were they to turn. The expertise came in the running of the office arrived in the person of my Grandpa Samuel. If you had searched the entire planet you could not of have found a more unlikely candidate to fill the role of comptroller.

With Grandpa firmly in control of the fish stores finances and Junior behind the counter serving the general public there was the wholesale side of the business to be attended too. My Dad assumed the mantle of the growth of outside sales of City Fish and Poultry Ltd.

The fish store did a good business on the wholesale side. They could name to their customer list many of the finest eating establishments and high end clubs in the city of Hamilton and a few in the Toronto area. The Royal Connaught Hotel, The Royal York Hotel, The Royal Hamilton Yacht Club to name just a few of the royalty that my Dad hung out with. One of his favorite customers were the guys at the Pagoda Restaurant. My Father would save this service call for the last of the day. And with good reason! They would sit in the kitchen amongst the yelling of the waiters and the clatter of pots. The smoke and grease being sucked up through giant fans that exhausted into the atmosphere from giant stainless flat top grills and huge vats of oil and rows of woks with cooks sweating and working the contents of their huge wash tub like pots. Chinese dishes of every variety would be whisked out a one way door to the Chinese enchanted gardens in the main dining room. Inside the kitchen they would drink. The owner of the Pagoda liked my Dad and treated him with great respect. My Dad enjoyed the company of his Chinese friends and would spend many an hour shooting the breeze and drinking their good and plentiful whiskey.

My Dad took me there once. I had been down town and had walked to the fish store hoping to catch a ride home. He said "okay, but we have to make a stop at a customer on the way home. I'll be awhile." Originally he wanted me to wait in the car for him but I begged him to let me come with him and he finally relented. "You have to promise that if they give you anything to eat you don't ask what it is, you just eat it. Do you promise?"

"I promise."

We went through the back doors and were suddenly standing in what appeared to be Chaos City. A little Chinese man in a white shirt with a tie that resembled a shoe lace and open at the collar spotted my Dad in the back and waved frantically for him to come forward to where he was standing. There was a large wooden table covered with small tea pots and white bowls of half eaten rice and other vegetables. The man clapped his hands loudly and an old Chinese woman seemed to appear out of nowhere, she quickly cleared and wiped the table. Chairs were repositioned as a more formal atmosphere settled around the table. "And whooo is tis wittle man you bling to my estabrishment?" I liked this man immediately. "This, Mr. Wong, is my number two son, John."

"Goood evaning Master John."

"Hello Mr. Wong" I thrust out my hand in an exaggerated manner, the gesture was received approvingly. Mr. Wong shook my hand while turning his head towards my Father with a big smile on his face. "Sit down, Sit down my flends. Whaaat can I get flor yooou?" "Nothing' said my Dad, "I just stopped by to see if everything was honky dory"

"evlything honkey doly. Ret's have a dlink. Whaaat wooourd yooou rike John?"

"I'll have a Coke please"

"Coooming light up." Mr .Wong clapped his hand and the old woman appeared. He said something completely unintelligible to the old Chinese ghost woman and she was gone. Reappearing with a hand full of Cokes and a bottle of Crown Royal, which she placed with great care, at the center of the table.

Glasses were issued to my Dad and Mr. Wong. The top popped off a bottle of Coke and placed in front of me. Mr. Wong nodded to me and then opened the Crown Royal and poured the glasses full of the golden rye whiskey. "Thele yooou go, Clown Loyal, ohnwee the best flor my flend."

"Whaaat wooourd yooou rike tooo eat" Remembering my

sworn promise to my Dad I didn't want to ask for anything specific so I said the only thing I could think of, "Oh, whatever you have." This was probably the dumbest thing I could have ever said to a guy who owned a Chinese restaurant while sitting in his kitchen. He grinned from ear to ear and yelled an order directed at one of the cooks who laughed heartily and yelled something back which caused all the cooks to laugh. A great commotion began. The cooks started to bang on their woks and yell all the while throwing pitiful glances at me. I felt as if I was about to be served a heaping plate of monkey poop, sautéed in hippopotamus snot all nestled on a bed of red worms. All the yelling and caring on by the cooks was a sign that they were thrilled to be making this order as it was not a frequently requested item on the menu.

Mr. Wong rose from his seat and raised his hand. The kitchen was silenced immediately. He clapped his hands once. The old Chinese woman appeared carrying a large tray with a silver tray warmer. Whatever monstrosity I was to be forced to eat was waiting for me under that silver dome. She handed the tray to Mr. Wong and he placed the tray before me. He had his hand on the dome. He stood to one side and said "Arrre yoooou leady." I nodded my head.

He ceremoniously pulled the dome off revealing... the best chocolate Sunday I was ever to eat.

The cooks and waiters broke into uproarious laughter. I suppose the look on my face had given away the trepidation I suffered while waiting for my meal.

After Mr. Wong and Dad had polished off the Clown Loyal and we were in the car heading for home my Dad said "you got off easy tonight."

"What'ya mean?"

"Well, when Mr. Wong pulled that stunt on me there was a big fish head under the dome"

"Did you eat it?" I asked, astonished that such a thing could even be possible. "Yep."

* * *

While Gramps may have handled the numbers of the store my Dad still handled the cash. Many are the nights, especially on Saturday nights my Father would arrive home with hundreds, perhaps thousands of dollars in a brown paper bag stuffed into the back pocket of his pants. Mom would pull her dramatic nonsense, "What are you going to do with all that money? Why didn't you drop it at the bank?" He would simply say "I'll put it in my bedside table drawer. The bank was closed before I had a chance to make the deposit." This last comment about the bank being closed was bullshit. Most stores that held cash until later in the evening and past the banks operating hours were equipped for night deposits. He had stopped for drinks somewhere on his way home and forgotten that his back pocket contained enough money that had any ill meaning person known about it they would have bashed in his head without a second thought.

* * *

The fish store was situated in a nineteen twenty eight brown stone building. Heating had never been installed and being that it was a fish store this was appropriate. During the spring and fall temperatures were moderated by Mother Nature and it was a pretty comfortable environment to work in. For the few hot summer months the iced down trays helped moderate the ambient temperature somewhat. The winter was another story. The place was freezing. If it was minus ten degrees outside, it was minus ten degrees inside. The only heat generated inside the store came from what the bodies would throw off that past in and out of the store and from a dinky little fan heater kept inside the pilot house office. It was one of those heaters that had a coiled element wrapped around a tin fan. The coil would glow red giving the impression that heat was being produced. The fan would blow the heat into the intended space at the equivalent BTU content of a match.

My Father would go to work wearing multiple layers of V neck sweaters to help keep him warm. Thick socks under heavy brogue shoes were all the protection he had for his feet against the cold. Nobody wore gloves in the store. Their hands, immersed in cold brine all day, were hard and corny. I once saw my Dad cut the fleshy palm of his hand just below the thumb. He was using one of the razor sharp filleting knives and he cut deep. Anybody else would have been bleeding like crazy and would have required several stitches to close the gash, his hand didn't even bleed. He casually acknowledged the cut like it was a minor annoyance and just kept on working without giving it a second thought. Besides, it was probably too cold for blood to flow.

I do not know who would have first thought about bringing a bottle of booze into the store as a way to ward off the cold but I am sure that it was, at first, an innocent action. One of those, we'll just have one drink to keep the chill off, ideas. Maybe it was late in the day, just before closing. A mickey would have been produced or perhaps it was just a flask that had been brought from home intending to warm the cockles of your heart after a freezing cold, hard day of work. Whatever, whoever, however, a dam had been breached and the flood of rye whiskey that was to come pouring in would drown them all.

In the back of the store facing the front door, was the office. It was built to replicate the pilot house of a vessel. Vertical two inch boards provided the support of three panes of glass looking out to the floor of the store. The bottom vertical boards were painted white and the framing wood on the windows were painted an odd shade of green. It was that green color that gas stations use to paint their washrooms. The office itself was probably no bigger than eight feet by eight feet. You entered the office at the end of the freezer cases from the side of the working area. There was a green steel desk and a tub style wooden office chair on wheels that didn't roll. The walls were a dark brown. At sometime there was a color but only nicotine stained walls were evident now. A telephone and a wire basket sat on the desk with today's orders and billings. In the center of the desk was a green desk blotter that had blotted all the blotting it was ever going to blot. Squatting against the back wall was a large, black metal safe that Jesse James and his brother Frank had tried to blow up and had failed. The door of the safe was open because nobody could remember the combination. They didn't need a safe anyway, they had Dad's back pants pocket.

On the inside of the office windows, the framing provided a two and one half inch ledge that ran all the way across the front of the windows.

Divine inspiration followed. Gramps measured up four inches from the ledge at the bottom of the window along the length of the windows. Painted a border in the ever popular gas station washroom green all along the window effectively blocking out any view of the first four inches into the office. Now comes the smart part. They would line up full shot glasses along the ledge of the window. When they wanted a snort they could just quickly duck around the corner. Fire back a shot of rye whiskey and return to their duties with nobody the wiser. Brilliant!

The luster of the brilliance began to tarnish as they began to load up the window ledges earlier and earlier each day. After the cold winter passed the practice continued into the warmer weather and eventually became just part of the everyday routine. They went from buying mickeys to quarts, obviously a time effective decision on the part of management and would certainly provide the customers with an improved level of service.

I was always bugging my Father to let me work at the store. Always curious to see what my old man did for a living. He was not having any of it. "You'll hate it, you're not strong enough, there's nothing for you to do." Then, one day, out of the blue my Dad asked me if I wanted to work at the store on Saturday. Apparently one of his swampers, he referred to them as ginks, had quit and there was a big semi truck coming in with a load of frozen halibut and he needed an extra hand. "Yeah, I'd love to, this will be great!"

"Yeah, we'll see how great come Saturday," was all he said.

At five o'clock on Saturday morning my Father was at the side of my bed, "get up, it's time to go." It was still dark outside. I trundled down stairs, ate some puffed wheat, grabbed the two lunches sitting in the fridge that Mom had made for us the night before and followed him outside to the car. It was still dark outside. I had never known my Mother to make my Father a lunch before. We hopped into the Pontiac and he told me to put the lunch bags in the back seat. Off we went, the men of the house going into the fields together to earn a living for the family by the sweat of our brows. It was still dark outside when we arrived at the taxi stand on the corner of James and Cannon streets where the City Fish and Poultry business rented space for their delivery trucks and Junior and Dad's cars.

We entered the alley off Cannon Street and entranced the store by the rear door, "careful, the trap door is open." "Whats the trap door for?" I asked anxiously. "It goes down to the basement," he said with a where do you think it goes attitude in his voice. "What's in the basement?"

"Compressors for the freezer cases and the cat."

"Why do you have a cat in the basement?" Knowing I was about to step over the stupid question line and spoil the whole day. My Dad seemed to back off the attitude and told me that they kept a big orange cat that kept the mice down. The cat didn't eat fish although he was fond of raw shrimp. During the day they would keep the cat in the basement and before they left the store at night they would open the trap door and the cat would have the run of the place. "Do you want to go down?"

"Sure."

The steps leading down to the basement were steep. The basement was as big as the store. No walls or bulkheads. Three rough wooden stages supported three compressors spaced evenly in a line going forward from the steps. The walls were rock. They reminded me of something you might see in a fort. Behind the steps was a toilet on another wooden platform just big enough to provide room for a person to mount the platform and sit with your feet close in to the base of the toilet. I was surprised to see that the toilet was in use. Sitting on the edge of the toilet was the cat having a shit looking rather indignant at this stranger that invaded her morning ablutions. I ascended the steps and while my head was still rising through the hole in the floor I yelled to my Dad, "Do you know that the cat is taking a poop on the toilet?"

"Yep."

The semi truck came in about seven o'clock and pulled along Cannon Street until the end of the truck was about even with the alley way. I was there waiting with my Dad, ready to do my part. The huge doors swung open and were clipped to the sides and the driver jumped up into the back. I realized it was colder in the truck than it was out in the morning fall air. The driver disappeared into an ice fog and reappeared pushing a fork lift with a pallet loaded with whole frozen halibut. They were stacked and wired down to the pallet and when the driver cut the straps they spilled out onto the floor of the truck.

I had never seen a whole halibut. Fortunately, these halibut were missing their heads. We took them, one at a time, from the back of the tractor trailer, up the alley and into the large freezer building located behind the store. Each one of these suckers weighed about sixty pounds. You would cradle the fish in the U shaped area where the head use to be with one hand and put your hand under the tail. Lean back and let your chest take the balanced weight. Well that's what you did if you were five foot eight. If you were five feet you rested the balanced weight of the fish against your forehead. It wasn't long before my head had frozen and my hands were of little more value than hooks intended to hang fish from.

My Dad carried a couple of fish up the alley and into the freezer unit, a kind of instructional period for my benefit then was gone. I worked my ass off unloading those fucking fish all that morning. I finished just before noon. The teamster looked down at me from the end of the trailer and simply said, "You done good kid." He went into the store to complete some paper work with my Dad. They went into the office and each took a shot glass from the ledge. Toasted each other, glanced at me, laughed and slung back the whiskey.

My Dad told me to come into the office where it was warmer. My uncle Junior came in about the same time with a large brown paper bag that smelt wonderful. The bag had grease running down the outside. They cleared the big green desk and tore open the brown bag. Then they carefully unwrapped the newspaper and its contents. "Halibut and chips for lunch dig in" said Dad. I had never figured my Father to be a sophisticate humorist. Ten tons of halibut carried and stored by me all morning and here he was serving halibut for lunch. I chalked it up to coincidence.

The remainder of the day was spent stacking smoked eels, literally like stacking cord wood and learning about the different kinds of fish, they referred to the fish as product.

Saturday was the busiest day of the week. People of all nationalities and creeds were fish buyers. Italians, Polish, Jewish, Chinese, Greek, Japanese, Spanish, Portuguese and my uncle Junior had a slang name for all of them. The product must have been exceptional because all these people, who supported our families through their purchases, took such shit and abuse from Junior, I was amazed. As the day wore on and the drinking and cold penetrated both mind and body my uncle's abuse grew to epic proportions.

Some customers would leave the store in disgust others would weather the prejudicial storm, few ever challenged because when they did he would simply tell them to get out and never come back. In those days when there was a feast or a holy day to be celebrated you didn't screw around with the main ingredient on the menu. They endured his obnoxious behavior.

Finally, after all the fish had been stored, all the trays had been washed, all the freezer cases wiped down, the tills emptied, the money counted and placed securely in a brown paper bag and stuffed into the back pocket of my Dad's pants, finally, it was time to close up shop and head for home. I would never have admitted to my Dad that I could hardly wait to get out of that place but I could hardly wait to get out of that place.

We pulled into the driveway at around six thirty and before we got out of the car Dad said, "Get the lunches out of the back seat." I got the lunches and we walked up the driveway to the back door. Dad stopped, took the brown bags from me, and opened the galvanized garbage can that sat in the driveway and dropped both bags into the can and replaced the lid. He didn't say a word and neither did I.

* * *

I suppose my apprenticeship into the world of fish mongering had been successful because when it came time for the Christmas rush Dad asked if I would come and work at the store on the Saturday before Christmas. He said he had some fish that needed scaling. I agreed, although I was not as excited as I had been before my first experience. I had a taste, so to speak, of the retail fish trade and it was not very spicy. Anyway, how hard could it be to weigh some fish?

This was the busiest day of the year. Jewish Hanukkah and the Christian Christmas all came together in one cataclysmic fish dish. For example the Italians had their traditional twenty four meatless dishes on Christmas Eve. That's a lot of fish when you consider that the Italian population in Hamilton was second only to New York City outside of Europe. Many other ethnic groups had similar celebrations and restrictive foods at that time of year and those meals featured fish. Even though Europeans were the big fish consumers, many Canadians enjoyed their seafood dishes consisting of shrimp, oysters, clams, crab and lobster.

The store had an exceptionally large order of a fish, some kind of white fish that was popular this time of year. This fish had scales and they had to be removed before they were displayed on the trays in the counter freezer cases. They didn't need to be weighed they needed to be scaled, as in stripped off.

I had never ever removed a single scale from a single fish in my entire life but by the end of that day I would have removed millions. To manually remove fish scales you use a steel oval cup, scalloped at the edges. You slide your hand between the cup and a metal band. It looks exactly like a horse brush minus the bristles. Fish scales are made of an enamel type substance and can be as hard as a human tooth.

In the back of the fish store along the wall are two huge square stainless steel tubs. Into the tubs go guts, heads, tails, bones, shells, and more guts. Everything that is not to be seen by the buying public and taken out the front door but has come in through the back door. This is to be the receptacle of my labor. Dad said, "You hold the fish by the tail and you begin to scrub the scales off starting at the tail and working forward to the head. Make sure that you get every scale. You got it? Here you try one." Nice, 6:20 in the morning and I have a cold fish by the ass end. Every time I stroke against the side of the fish the scales pop off and fly about me. I know they are in my hair and stuck on my face. I try to remove them. "Don't worry about that, you'll be covered with them soon anyway. Put some elbow grease into it." I finish my practice fish and we step outside to confront what essentially is a white plastic hot tub sized container of fish. "And when you finish this tub there's another one. Let me know when you're getting low and I'll get one of those ginks to replace it." As he points to the drivers who are smoking in the alley way. I think to myself how inspiring and motivational it must be to work around here, and then realize I am working around here.

A gink is just a guy who probably should have finished high school. A normal guy, trying to make a living and gets a job as a pick up truck driver, delivering fish on behalf of the City Fish and Poultry. It doesn't take an exceptional group of skill sets to perform these duties, a chauffeur's driver's license, a reasonable geographic knowledge of the city and an affinity for rye whiskey will suffice. One of these ginks is actually a neighbor's kid, a few years older than I am who had clearly not set his sights high enough and wrangles a job driving truck. I like this guy and I'm surprised to see him working here. Not as surprised as he is to see me working here. I greet him with our regular salutation, "Howdy pots"

"Howdy pans." Something he taught me and we have continued to use it for many years. This doesn't impress my old man in the least. Two minutes on the job and I'm already speaking gink.

I begin my scaling of the fish. The fish average about twenty four inches long and have a girth of maybe nine inches. They have their heads on but have been gutted so they do not have much substance and are difficult to support when you are trying to put pressure on them in order to put some elbow grease into them. I begin to get a rhythm and soon my mind wanders and fantasizes about many different scenarios. I realize that men on a chain gang must use mental games to get through their day.

Before I know it I'm calling for my Dad to get those ginks to get me a second tub of fish. In my fantasy I have imposed mermaid like qualities on the fish. I am not scaling fish from some cold northwest lake any more but rather stripping the clothes off mermaids from some warm southwest tropical island.

At sometime through the day my Dad tells me to take a break. "Get into the office and get warm and have some lunch." Ah lunch! I have completely forgotten about lunch. From the time it takes me to cross from my semi permanent position at the stainless steel tubs to enter the office, approximately three steps, and my mind conjures up sitting down to some hot tomato soup with maybe a nice gooey grilled cheese sandwich to go with it. That thought shatters as I spy a pile of hamburgers in individual wrappings just heaped on the center of the desk. I dig in and it may not be the dream I had hoped for but the burgers are delicious all the same. Looking around for something to wash the burger down with I see a half a dozen or so full shot glasses but that's about it. I guess the management had forgotten about the forced child laborer and the fact that he might get thirsty too. I look about for a cup or a glass and realize that they do not own a glass taller than two inches. I grab an empty shot glass and go over to the stainless steel tub. I am in the process of rinsing the shot glass and drinking my fill from this tiny vessel when I glance down into the ooze lying in the bottom of the tubs. Perhaps I don't need a drink after all.

I continue with my defrocking of the fish until once again I scrape the bottom of the barrel. I 'm actually finished, call Guinness. I am sure I am the new world record holder for fantasies involving fish. I am congratulated by some of the ginks which is nice however, the co-commandants of the camp give no indication of approval. The thought crosses my mind that perhaps Hermann Melville worked here just before he wrote Moby Dick. The store itself taking on the characteristics of the great white whale, cruising the oceans of the world alone and in silence for all eternity. Captain Ahab, a composite character of the brothers, Junior and Glenn in a never ending life quest to kill the white whale.

I ask my Dad," where's all the fish I scaled?" and he shows me a couple of trays, the rest having gone out the front door at sixty cents a pound.

It is still fairly early in the day so I am given another job, a kind of search and destroy mission. This involves sole fillets. I didn't know, and still do not want to know, that sole have this nasty little habit of picking up little white worms along the flesh in their sides. The little parasites set up housekeeping in their hosts by making themselves at home and helping themselves to the flesh of the fish. A good fish monger knows this and removes the little pest neatly and discreetly.

The sole fillets themselves come in a plastic tub twenty four inches by fourteen inches and eight inches deep. Above the stainless steel tub two one hundred watt bulbs that do double duty. The first is obvious the second is a sort of X-ray for fish. If you hold the fillet up to the light the shadow of the curled up worm will appear. It is then simply a matter of taking one of the razor sharp filleting knives from the rack and delicately cutting out the tiny invader. The operation leaves no trace and the customer gets a nice clean fillet. After performing this maneuver a thousand times I have sworn off sole forever.

The day wears on; the customers are now lined up outside the door. The line goes to the corner and continues along Cannon Street. The liquor store has been visited several times by now, the ginks have been adding this stop to their regular deliveries. Copious amounts of rye whiskey have been swallowed and there is an uneasy feeling building behind the service counter. This feeling seems to be emanating from Uncle Junior. Like a gunfighter just itching for a fight he is losing patience and looking for somewhere or someone to unload on. The target for the first firing of verbal bullets comes in the form of a little Japanese man who falters in his speech when asked brusquely, "What'aya want?" Junior being as eloquent as ever. The poor man hesitates and stammers and that is all that Junior needs to unload on this guy. "Obviously we didn't drop enough bombs on you little Jap shits." I can't believe the insults and abuse that comes out of Junior's mouth. Everyone unfortunate enough to be served, if service is what you could call it, by Junior gets a side order of racial slurs thrown in for free. My Father ignores him and continues on with dealing as pleasantly as possible with the customers who are beginning to shove over to avoid Junior's line up. The Jewish don't need to be reminded of the holocaust, the Italians have been trying to forget Mussolini and the Canadians can't believe that their Father's or a Brother may have given their lives so this asshole could sell fish.

The ginks are paid off and sent on their way. Junior and Glenn have to cut off the line arbitrarily. My father leaves this task to Junior who simply swears at the customer who protests about the closing. Almost eight o'clock. We have been standing in sub zero temperatures for fourteen hours. Our hands have been exposed to salt brine, spiny crustaceans, scaly fish and the freezing cold. I don't realize how beat I am until everything comes to a deafeningly quiet stop. We clean up the all the trays and store all the fish in the cooler out back. They get the money together, this time my father gets a banks night deposit bag out of the office desk drawer. They peel off a couple of hundred each and stuff the bills into their pockets. The rest of the money, and there is a lot, gets counted and recorded neatly on a deposit slip and put into the gray bankers bag. We lock up the store and cross the street to the parking lot. It is snowing now and the streets are quiet. It is Christmas Eve. We drive up to the bank with the bag of money on the seat between us. Dad pulls the car over to the night deposit repository, drops the bag in through the slot and we are off again heading for home. We drive along in silence. We are just too tired to even speak. I can't help myself and I ask, "How come Uncle Junior is so prejudice and you're not?"

"When I was a kid and I was boxing I had to fight a Negro. He was the toughest kid I ever fought but I beat him. I had a lot of respect for that Negro kid and it just stuck with me." It was the most articulate explanation of anything I had and would ever hear come out of my Fathers mouth.

Aside from painting a four inch green border around the window ledge of the office in order to conceal the shot glasses that provided everyone who worked in the store with a daily glow my Grandpa Clark took care of the books. He actually did have an accounting background. Previous to his illustrious career as the City Fish comptroller and painter he had been engaged by the Toronto, Hamilton and Buffalo, rail lines as a ticket agent. Also known as the TH&B Railway. As kids we thought TH&B stood for tramps, hobos and bums. Working for City Fish certainly gave my Gramps an outlet for his more creative side.

When Gramps died of cancer we lost a great character. One who had entertained us with his humor and his sax. The store lost its bookkeeper. They never replaced him. Perhaps the thought of interviewing to fill that position was a little taunting for Junior and Glenn to contemplate. How you would write the job advertisement would have certainly posed some problems.

Bookkeeper wanted. Must like rye whiskey. Being able to work in an environment of sub zero temperatures an asset. Being able to withstand verbal abuse and racial slurs would be helpful but on the job training is available. If you do not mind smelling like a mackerel this career is for you.

Conducting an interview in itself would prove to be an ordeal that neither of them chose to contemplate. Unless they were lucky enough to attract an alcoholic accountant who was a hermit, the chances of filling the position was slim to none.

So with no real prospects to fill the position of bookkeeper my Father assumed the responsibility for the stores financials.

The brothers hold to their course. The store provides for the three partners, one silent, deep in the glades of Florida while the other two continue to work the daily grind.

THINGS GO SIDEWAYS

While the kids were growing up and out there was something beginning to change with my Father and it was not the change most other people were experiencing in the sixties. Something sinister, something way down deep in the core of his mind was changing. It was subtle and slow. Because he drank so much, by now he was a functioning alcoholic; it was hard to distinguish this change in behavior from his regular gassed up routines.

But the worm in his mind was turning, turning, turning.

* * *

While Dad had never been a social butterfly he could navigate through a party of friends and acquaintances. For the most part he appeared to be enjoying himself. As long as there was booze he could tolerate most situations. I had only known him to pass out from drinking twice in my life.

Every couple of years there was a family reunion held by some distant relation. On this particular occasion Elizabeth and I accompanied my Mom and Dad to the reunion. I did not know how I was related to them but they were nice folks. They had a hobby farm just outside of Hamilton. A property that held the house and a small barn. There were some fruit trees and a garden patch. They had put in a putting green beside the barn and there was a tee box where you could drive balls out into a field. The festivities were held in the barn. It had been redecorated for fun occasions. There was a juke box providing the music and generating a little atmosphere from its meager light show. A piano that by the end of the day had someone inspiring a sing along. All the adults, who by that time had consumed plenty of liquid courage would know the words and the tunes and would sing their hearts out.

Everyone would bring something for the picnic style meal. Fried chicken and potato salad were my favorites. These two items were duplicated many times over and it was at this table I learned the secret of life. There is no such thing as bad fried chicken, just some are better. You could eat your fill of salads, fresh vegetables of every kind. Beautiful pies filled with apples, peaches, strawberry and rhubarb, and cherry. Truly a treasure trove of tasty treats for the taking.

The adults reveled on through the afternoon and into the evening. The conversation, as always, turned to the folks who were not there. And the remember so and so stories would take over. A tear or two for good measure and the party would begin to break up. No one had noticed that my Dad was not in attendance. In fact it had been quite a while since anybody remembered seeing him. Highly unusual behavior for stalwart Glenn. Of course a search ensued and he turned up, well not up, on the putting green. He had passed out, but not before puking in the green's hole. A lot of hole in one jokes were used to cover up my families obvious embarrassment at the situation. With a great amount of assistance from many helping hands we were able to deposit my Father in the back seat of the family Pontiac were he promptly returned to unconsciousness.

We said our goodbyes and we gave our apologies and with Elizabeth and Mom in the front seat, Dad snoring to beat the band in the backseat and me behind the wheel, we headed off for home. I didn't even have a driver's license. We pulled into the driveway and I asked my Mom what to do with Dad? "Leave him" she said. And we did.

I have no idea when he woke up or what happened when he did. As usual in our family, the way we dealt with situations of that kind, no one said anything.

A similar situation had taken place a few years earlier only this time it was my older brother who had driven the family home.

My parents were visiting with some friends who had a cottage on the beach up at Long Point and Dad had managed to drink himself into a state of unconsciousness. It was an hour and a half of driving to get home and by the time we arrived my Father was beginning to stir. We managed to get him into the house and onto the bed. The next morning the car was in the driveway. It was the only time I ever knew my Dad to miss a day of work.

One of the most disturbing alcohol related events fortunately did not involve any of the kids. My mother told me about it the following morning Father.

One of my friends whose Father ran a realty investment business was opening a new office and asked me if I could put together a quartet to provide some background music at his grand opening. I grabbed our rhythm guitar player and bassist and we put together some numbers that were popular at the time and would be mood music for this gig. My friends Father invited my Parents to the opening as a courtesy. No obligation, just a couple of drinks and they could enjoy the music. It was the regular boring evening, brush strokes on a snare drum to the beat of Girl from Uponema.

My Father was spending a lot of time at the free bar and was beginning to swirl and slur. They finally cut him off and he and my Mother head for home.

"Well," she started with the dramatics, "We headed for home, and I knew he was a little drunk but I didn't think he didn't know where he was. We drove right past the turn to our street. I said Glenn, where are you going? He said he was going home. I told him that he had missed the turn and he looked at me like I was nuts."

"So where did he take you?" I was a little amused at this stage.

"He drove all the way to our old house on the beach strip. He had it in his head that that is where we lived. He kept trying to get out of the car and going in the old house. It took me an hour to convince him that we lived on Aldous. Finally he gave in but I had to give him directions to the house. It was the damnedest thing."

"So what happened when you guys got home?"

"Nothing, you know your Father, he just went to bed." I was a bit frustrated with the standard don't address the situation bullshit. "This sounds pretty serious to me. Maybe it's time to address the drinking issue, maybe it's time to get some help, some professional help."

" Oh, I don't think we have to do that. I could never get him to go and get help anyway."

"So, you're just going to leave it?"

"Well, yeah, I guess so, for the time being."

He began to go to bed earlier and earlier. There became less of a routine to follow. He would get up at five AM, go to work, come home, and have a couple of drinks and go to bed around eight o'clock. Little socializing, if any, little conversation, no enthusiasm generated for anything. He was becoming an automaton.

Dad became obsessed with Elizabeth. Constantly referring to her as young Elizabeth and always concerned for where and what she was doing. We would be visiting with an Aunt and Uncle and he would insist on leaving early so that young Elizabeth could get to bed. On his days off he would constantly be asking about her whereabouts. She could be at some neighbors place playing with a girlfriend and he would be regularly checking on her. It wasn't that he wanted to know anything or even do something when he had whatever information it was that he was seeking. He just needed to check on young Elizabeth. It became such a tiring and recurring event that we would tease Elizabeth, referring to her as young Elizabeth. I thought that he was using her as his alibi, to cover for his behavior.

I tried to get Mom to have him checked out by a Doctor but she was not interested in going that route. She just figured that he was tired, had lost interest in her and lost interest in life in general.

That summer all hell broke loose. After Gramps had died and My Dad had taken over the responsibilities of the fish stores books no one was checking anything. Nobody thought to check on my Fathers bookkeeping expertise. Even though there was ample evidence that my Father was sick no one took the precaution of taking a closer look at the finances of City Fish. And no one would ever know what happened to the three hundred thousand dollars that went unaccounted for.

Dad wasn't saying anything. Whether he did not even give it any attention or he knew things were going sideways and was not about to be up front, he wasn't talking. I suppose it must have started with creditors. One by one the suppliers were starting to call looking for payment.

I would imagine in the beginning the creditors would call and if they were talking to Dad they would be asking for their payment. He would have probably said, "Yep." There would have been no reason for them to be nervous. For the past twenty years they had received their money on time, with never a hassle. And another week or so would go by. They would make another call and maybe this time they would get Junior who would have said, "I'll leave a message for Glenn to get back to you." Junior would pass the message on, or have left a note on the desk and another week or so would go by. Junior might show a little initiative and ask a question or two on the status of the stores finances of his Brother. To which he would receive a reply of either "Nope" or "Yep." If that satisfied his curiosity maybe Bernia and Percival's cheques were not showing up on time, or maybe they had stopped receiving their money altogether. It's quite possible the store cash register ran dry. It may have been as simple as they were going to get a bottle of rye and when they went to the petty cash there was none, but somehow City Fish and Poultry Ltd. were broke.

Junior made a few futile attempts at establishing the problem. His years of neglect and frivolous attitude toward the affairs of the business were coming home to roost. He did not have a clue where to begin to look let alone what to look for.

Bernia and Percival chose to make the drive up from Florida. The old warhorse will get to the bottom of all this Tom Foolery.

What Bernia doesn't realize is that old Tom Foolery is now Mr. Tom Foolery and he is not kidding around. There is no money.

She lets her son know that she will be arriving for a meeting at Aldous for seven o'clock after he gets home from the store. He had better have some answers for her.

Dad and Mom are sitting on the front porch under the green awning having a rye and Pepsi. They look absolutely oblivious to the reality of the situation. And why not? No doubt the first Mom ever heard of the stores financial troubles was from Junior and chances are he wasn't making much sense. I am around the side of the house. I don't know what's going to happen but I am a more concerned than Mom and Dad who are sitting on the porch. Mom prattles on to her husband about not letting his Ma bully him into anything. "Stand up for yourself. You have given your life to that store. It's only because of you that she and Percival can live in Florida in the lap of luxury."

The yellow Buick Skylark with the plastic seat covers comes to a halt across the street. Bernia bolts from the car to the foot of the porch steps, Percival lagging behind. Dad looks down at his Mother with a surprised expression and cheerfully says, "Hi Ma." Bernia loses it right there. "I have just come from the accountants and the store is out three hundred thousand dollars. So Laddie where is it?" Dad does not answer but he does stop grinning at her. "You must know what you have done?"

"Nope."

Bernia is shaking, the color of a fire engine. Percival has positioned himself so as to catch her when she collapses, sure she is about to do at any moment. Bernia moves up another step and says. "There has not been a deposit in three months. You haven't collected money on any of the wholesale customers in four months. The only money is what's in the till. Listen boy, you had better tell me where the money is or I'm going to crack you in the head." Bernia moves up another step. Silence. He just stares at her. I have moved up to the bottom of the steps. Focused on her boy and the lack of reasonable answers to her questions she does not notice me. I can see my Father struggling, trying so hard not to let his Mother down. This may be the first time in his life she has ever had a reason to be disappointed in her boy. He struggles to make connections. Then the struggling disappears, he relapses to whatever corner of his brain he usually lives in and smiles at her. Bernia mounts the last step and begins to beat her son with her fists. Flailing away like the wings of a moth against a dull light bulb. She bursts into tears and Percival and I drag her off Dad. Blubbering and muttering incoherently, truly spent. She pulls away from me with a nasty shrug and some rude remark about the bitches litter. Percival half carries her back to the Buick. They leave. The last board meeting of the City Fish and Poultry Corporation has concluded.

* * *

I look in the trunk of the Pontiac to see if Dad had been depositing the money there. He hadn't. It wasn't three hundred thousand dollars that was missing, well not in cash. No one will ever know what was invoiced and how much of that ever came back. Dad wasn't paying any bills at the time so they would have got hit pretty hard when they started up again. It is true that there would have been a lot of cash unaccounted for. All the money taken in over the counter and all moneys that would have been picked up by the drivers from customers who would have chosen to send along payments with the return drivers. It was a different time and people did business in different manner than today.

At a bank somewhere between James Street and Aldous Avenue there was teller who could never get his night deposits to balance. The cash would always tally higher than the deposit slips allowed for. At that stage of Dad's illness he would never have the mental faculties to distinguish one bank from another. Wherever there was a night depository and it was convenient, that would have been the recipient of a cash award. Unless he was just throwing out the money with the trash, which was also possible. I suppose we will never really know what happened to all that money.

HIDE THE KEYS

"Your Uncle Junior phoned from the store today to tell me that your Father has been running into taxi cabs and driving away." This is what greets me one day when I get home from school. "Tomorrow I want you to go up to the store after school and ride home with your Father and see what's going on."

Dad has been mentally going downhill quite steadily but still you can't get my Mother to make a medical move.

I question my Dad later that evening, "Junior says that you ran into a couple of taxis on the lot and that you just drove away. Is that true?"

"Yep," this had become the standard length of every sentence. You ask my Father anything and the answer he will mutter is Yep or Nope.

The next day I am on the bus after school to hook up with my Father and catch a ride home again while all the time acting as an observer to assess my Dad's driving skills. My Dad's in the tiny office, Junior is by the stainless steel tubs cleaning up some trays. "What's this about Dad running into some taxi cabs on the lot?"

"Exactly!" Junior is in a foul mood, more so than normal. "A couple of weeks ago he backed into a taxi while leaving the parking lot to go home. He smacked right into the side of one and then just drove away. There was a driver in the cab so there wasn't any question as to who had hit the taxi. Then, two nights ago he did the same thing. I can't keep settling up with these guys from the stores till. You're going to have to do something."

"What do you think we should do?" I was hoping to get a little input from his brother. "Well how should I know?" Nice contribution. Thanks for the input. I get my Father and we head out across street to the parking lot.

The parking lot is just a crushed gravel lot situated on the corner of James Street. It is a one way street running north to south. Cannon Street is another one way street. It's traffic running from east to west. The lot is just large enough to hold a small taxi shack and half a dozen cabs. The delivery trucks for City Fish are parked in this lot along with my Uncles and Father's car. There is an entrance off Cannon Street but no barrier's or fencing run around the perimeter of the property.

We get into the Pontiac and Dad starts the car. Like he was pulling the arm on a slot machine he slams the column shift selector into Drive and off we go. We go across the sidewalk. We go over the curb. We are now heading east on a west bound one way street. And it doesn't faze him in the least. I am yelling, "What the fuck are you doing?" This should have elicited some response. "Stop the car! Pull over! Your gonna get us killed!" This gets a response, he laughs. People are blowing their car horns. They are swerving and heading for either curb because we are barreling down the center lane the wrong way. He finally makes a right hand turn onto Sherman Avenue. At least we are going with the traffic. The reprieve does not last long as he makes a left hand turn, through a red traffic light onto King Street. I can't believe we haven't hit anybody or that someone hasn't hit us. I am trying to navigate and calculate in my mind what the odds may be of making it home alive. I figure they are not good. We make a hard left onto Aldous. Just two more blocks and we are home. I quick right into the driveway, he turns the ignition off while the car is still rolling, slams the transmission into park and hops out headed for the house. I look at the dashboard and I realize we did all this in the dark without the headlights on.

I stagger from the passenger seat down the driveway and wonder how the in the hell he has managed not to kill himself or anybody else. I know he has been getting worse but this is an eye opener of gigantic proportions.

"Well, how did he do? Were there any problems with his driving?"

"Mom we need to take the keys away from him right now. It's hard to believe he has made it this far." I relate the highlights of our driving adventure. "Oh, you're exaggerating. It couldn't have been that bad."

"If you continue to allow him to drive someone will be seriously hurt."

"Well, you're just going to have to drive him to work every morning." I couldn't believe what she was saying. I don't think she knew what she was saying. "How am I going to take him to work and go to school and then come home from school and pick him up from work every night? Are you nuts?"

"If you don't take him to work how will we live? How will he get paid?" I can't believe we are having this conversation. My Dad gets up a 5:00 AM and leaves the store at 6:00 in the evening. I am searching for some practical solution, something normal. "Don't they have any disability insurance? He is a partner in the business, there must be some protection for his family in the event of a disability." My mother insists that he must be taken to work and that there is no provision for a disabled partner's family. Then she says that I am to get up in the morning and drop him off at work, come home and park the car, walk to school, walk home, get the car and then go and pick him up. "In another life." I say.

I tell her that we have a bigger hurtle. Getting the keys from Dad and having him cooperate with being driven by me. "You know he will not stand for his car being taken away and me driving him."

"We will just have to make it clear to him that that is the way things are going to have to be from now on. "You tell'em," she says.

I sit down with Dad at the table as he is shoveling down his supper. Head down, looking directly at the plate, arm and hand working together like moving a load of manure. "Ya' know Dad, you didn't do too well on the drive home this evening,"

"Yep."

"I think tomorrow I'll do the driving for you."

"Yep."

Somewhere in his brain he knew, and was relieved that he was off the hook. Somehow he knew that getting out from behind the wheel was the best thing for him. I always got a kick out of the times he exhibited these little glimmers of reason. I don't know where they lived in his brain but I was truly glad they were there.

The next morning I was up and in the kitchen at 5:00 AM. Dad ate two bowls of Corn Flakes and we were out the door. Without any prompting he sat in the passenger's seat. We arrived at the store and I dropped him off at the alley. He went up the alley to the back door of the store and I took off for home and maybe an hour of sleep before school. Foolishly I did not set my alarm and slept in. I was going to be late for school. Just perfect! I grabbed my books and headed for the car. I just might make it if I drove to school. When I got home from school there was Mom doing her foot tapping pissed off routine. "I told you to walk to school and not to take the car."

"I was late for school so I took the car. I didn't see you in the kitchen at

5:00 o'clock this morning. If you don't want me to drive Dad you get a license and do it yourself." She didn't bug me about it after that.

* * *

I left to go get Dad at around five thirty in the afternoon. He was standing at the end of the alley waiting. He got in the car and I realized he had shit himself. "What the hell is going on? Why did you poop in your pants? Why didn't you use the can in the store?"

"Junior wouldn't let me." was all he said. "I'll talk to Junior in the morning," fucking Junior!

All the way home I kept trying to think up ways to handle this situation. I knew that when we walked through the door Mom was going to have a figurative shit. There was no easy way around this. The best defense is a strong offense "Dad had an accident in his pants. Run a bath for him and help him out of those clothes." Then I turned around and left the house for the rest of the evening.

The next morning, same routine, two bowls of Corn Flakes at

five in the morning then off to the store. This time we went in together. Junior was just taking his coat off when we came through the door. He had a surprised look on his face when he saw me. "My Dad says that you wouldn't let him use the can in the basement, how come?"

"We were real busy and I didn't have time to get to the trap door before he put a load in his pants." To me, it sounded like he had rehearsed this story. "Ah come on, how busy can you be?"

"You don't know what it's like in here and just how busy it can get."

"I've been here when it was plenty busy. I think you could show your brother a little courtesy." I could see the color rising in his face. He didn't like what I had said but he gathered his thoughts and said, "It won't happen again, I'll make sure he can use the toilet any damn time he wants."

"Thanks," I said and was gone.

* * *

Just as had been the case when we were getting up in the mornings as children and fending for ourselves I am sure my Father had never had a cup of coffee made for him except on rare occasions. It was a cold February morning. And damned if this wasn't going to be one of those rare occasions.

I came into the kitchen as usual expecting to see my Father standing by the kitchen sink, eating his way through his Corn Flakes. Instead there was my Mother making two cups of instant coffee. Oh fuck! Lit up inside my head in an array of bright colors. "I thought I would get up and see my men off to work." "Okay." I said, trying to breathe naturally. "I think I'll just go outside and start the car to warm it up," it's all I could think of to get me out of the house. I waited in the car and I waited in the car and then I waited some more. Dad and I had a routine that worked well for us and we didn't need anyone messing it up. I was just about to go back in the house to get him when he came around the corner. I started to laugh. No it wasn't laughter, I was hysterical. I did not think it was possible to laugh that hard at five o'clock in the morning. There was Father standing in the beams of the car's headlights in an overcoat and a toque with a pom-pom on the top. My Dad had never worn a hat of any kind. I would bet that the last time my Father ever wore a hat was when he was in the Air Force. He climbed into the passenger seat and sat there. Although my Dad wasn't talking much anymore the look on his face spoke volumes. We backed out of the driveway and started up the street. I felt bad for him because every time I looked over at him I would burst out into laughter. "Do you want to wear that hat to work?" "Nope." "Why don't you put that hat in the backseat?"

"Yep." He whipped it off and tossed it into the back seat.

When we pulled into the driveway that night I told him to get the hat and put it on. "I don't feel like hearing one of those I don't know why I bother to try speeches from Mom"

"Yep." He said, which made me chuckle. I went ahead through the door without looking back to see if he had put the hat on. We came into the kitchen and the first thing my Mother said was "Where's your hat?" I jumped in with "it must be in the car. I'll go and get it." I wanted to put this to rest as quickly as possible and without any hassles. I looked in the car, it wasn't there. I looked up and down the driveway, it wasn't there. A smile came over my face, just in case, I lifted the lid on the garbage can. There was the stupid hat with the pom-pom on the top. I took it back into the house and said" I found it," directing the statement towards my Dad. In one of those lucid moments that sometimes came over him he took the hat and said with all the satirical venom he could muster, "Thanks."

* * *

I pull up to the alley one evening, just another of our regular pickups, Dad gets in and we head for home. He is unusually quite this night. Not that he was ever a candidate for the president of

88

the semantics team. The regular Yeps and Nopes are absent from our conversation. We get into the house and Mom gives out a shriek, "you're bleeding." He had been bleeding from his ear lobe and it was a deep gash. I had not seen it because it was on the right side of his head away from my field of vision. I couldn't imagine how he could have possibly cut himself in the ear. I let Mom clean the cut and let Dad settle down to his supper. I gently prod him to answer my questions. I have learned through experience it is best not to shriek, yell and throw a fit if you are going to get any relevant information from my Father on any subject.

"So what happened to your ear? Were you gutting some fish and the knife slipped?"

"Nope"

"You didn't cut your ear did you?"

"Nope."

"How did your ear get cut?"

"Junior did it"

"You guys were fighting?"

"Yep."

I turn this scenario over in my mind a couple of times. These two brothers are having a knife fight in their fish store.

I am so fucking mad, fed up and pissed off with this shit, I could leave the whole mess and never look back. I feel so alone, I have no one to turn to for help or even to talk with about this insane situation. I go upstairs, I lie on my bed and don't even realize that I'm crying. I'm so fucked up I don't even know when I'm losing it. I collect myself and go back downstairs. "Dad, tomorrow morning I'll have a talk with Junior. Don't worry about anything, I'll take care of it."

Next morning I was still at slow boil. I rushed Dad through his Corn Flakes and we jumped into the car and headed for the store. Rather than use the alley as we normally did I opted for the front door. I did not wait for my Father to get out of the car, I bolted through the front door and there was Junior behind the counter with an astonished look on his face which was rapidly morphing into one of a scared rabbit. "I didn't do anything to him," he shouted. I hadn't even said anything yet, although I suppose my face had the whole story written plainly on it. I stepped forward and he made the most amazing move I did not think was possible. On the wall, above the cash register was a small shelf that held a porcelain clock. The numbers were replaced with the words EAT FISH OFTEN. Junior managed to scamper up the cash register and sat with his ass on the shelf and that became his point of refuge. If I wasn't as angry as I was I am sure the site would have sent me into fit of laughter. As it was, I knew the image of him leaping to his perch would be burned in my mind for all time. "Don't you ever touch him again!" That was all I could get out. I had planned to unload a diatribe of unparalleled eloquence but all I could say was don't you ever touch him again. Wow! I thought, that was original. That will go down as one of the great harangues of the century. Pissed off with Junior, pissed off with my own inadequate denunciation I turned to leave. There was Dad standing in the doorway looking up at his brother balanced on the little and shelf, a look of astonishment on his face. "Your brother is dusting," was all I said and I was gone.

* * *

It was a Saturday and I arrived at the store earlier than usual. I park the car in the taxi lot and cross Cannon Street. Up the alley and in through the back door. I am standing beside the stainless steel tubs. Junior glances back at me from behind the freezer case. His countenance is one of surprise. "I was running a couple of errands and decided to come by a little early. Where's Dad?"

"He's down in the basement." Well that's good I think to myself, he must be having a poop. Better there than in his pants. "I stand around for a few minutes stomping my feet to keep warm. Getting a little impatient I ask Junior, "How long has he been down there?"

90

"All day." says Junior.

"My Dad's been taking a crap for the whole day?"

"No." Junior sends me a don't be so stupid look and says, "That's where we keep him."

The realization of that statement, with all its implications literally stuns me.

I feel nauseas. My ears were pounding and my eyes can't seem to focus. I'm holding on to the stainless tub because I fear I may sink to my knees. I am trying desperately to comprehend what I have just heard. "What do you mean, that's where we keep him?" Without a hint of quilt or any sense of remorse he says to me "He can't do anything so to keep him out of the way I put him down in the basement."

"For how long?" "

"All day."

"You're telling me that you keep your own brother down in the basement because he is in the way?" A feeling of intense heat hits my face as I realize that they kept their Father down there when he was sick. That's why Junior doesn't think that treating his brother no better than the store cat is wrong. He is only doing what he was taught. "For how long?" "

"All day. I already told you"

"No, how long have you been doing this?"

"A month or so."

"Fucker."

"You had better watch your mouth young man, I'm still your uncle."

"Not anymore."

I open the trap door and there is my Dad sitting on an over turned plastic bucket. He still has his coat and gloves on from this morning. He has sat in the basement for twelve hours. For the past month he has sat in this basement for three hundred and sixty hours. Sat alone.

When we arrive home I am in a foul mood. I tell my Mom to get Dad some soup and to make him a big plate of bacon and fried eggs. This is one of his favorite meals. Mom doesn't argue or squabble. She sets about preparing my Dads meager feast. "Do you want to eat?"

"No thanks."

"Are you going to tell me what's wrong or will I have to guess?" "I shoot her a don't fuck with me glance and say, "We will talk after Dad has finished his supper and gone to bed. Then I will tell you everything."

We sit down at the kitchen table, I at one end, her at the other. She is drinking a Seagrams and Pepsi. As long as she doesn't get too many into her before we have finished it shouldn't do any harm, perhaps it will even prove medicinal. After relating all that has been going on with Junior and the store. I summarize the entire dialogue with, 'It's time to get him out of there." And here it comes. "How will we live? What will we do for money?"

"I don't know but we can't continue to let him stand in the basement of a fish store. There must be some cash somewhere. He is a partner in the store, that's got to be worth something. You will just have to talk to Junior and see what can be worked out."

Whatever she had said to Junior, she had managed to wrangle a hundred dollars a week out of him. I was to pick up the money every Saturday night just before closing time.

DEMENTIA

We were having a bar-b-Que We had a small group of friends and relatives over. Nothing special, some hamburgers, potato salad and beers. As usual, every one expressed the polite observation that Glenn wasn't himself. I do not know whether they made these comments out of genuine concern or the embarrassment they felt for not having attended to their friendship with our family because they were uncomfortable. Probably it was both.

Things went along as good as could be expected. Mom dressed in one of her outlandish kaftans fluttered about her guests like some giant multi colored butterfly. The friends and relatives would take their turns going over to Glenn and asking him how he was doing. He would give them that stare. Even though he was looking right at you, he was also looking right through you at the same time. It was an eerie look, quite unsettling and it usually brought a halt to the patronizing scenarios that each guest would perform. I liked to think that my Dad knew exactly what he was doing to people. It helped me to feel better that maybe he was still in control. Although I knew it was not the case I got a kick out of thinking he was able to get inside their heads and mess about.

Following their obligatory visit to my Father they would inevitably come over to me and with as much sincerity as they could possibly generate, they would lay a hand on my shoulder and say, "It's all up to you now, you're the man of house, take care of your mother and sister."

"Thanks for coming" I would say, even though I knew they had no plans to leave just yet I tried to give them a nudge out the door.

I know that these people meant well but they had no clue as to what went on in this house. My mother was barely in touch with reality. It wasn't that she didn't know what was real it's that she simply and completely chose to ignore it. She never ceased to amaze me at the way she could interpret events to suit her purposes. As she was fond of saying to friends, "Oh, one day Glenn will wake up and snap out of it."

Dad was standing on the porch holding a paper plate with some potato salad on it. He began to shake, first his extremities and then the shaking moved to his body core. It was violent. He just kept on trying to eat. He would try and shovel some potato salad on to his fork but he was shaking so vehemently that the potato salad would fly off his fork and splat against the wall. There were radishes and egg bits in his hair. I took the plate away, it would have been easier to take a bear cub from a sow than to take his food away from him. I tried to restrain him and at the same time not to hurt him. Who was I kidding he was still as strong as an ox. Nothing seemed to be able to stop his seizure. When it finally subsided on its own and he was back eating, like nothing had happened. I lost it.

I told my Mother that if she didn't arrange for a Doctor to look at him. I would leave. She would have no one to take care of him, her and Elizabeth. Then I stomped upstairs, sat on the edge of my bed and cried. The pressures and frustrations just poured out of me. I thought, this was truly an insane asylum and was one of its inmates.

* * *

Doctor Dye was the family GP and an appointment was set for a Friday afternoon.

I spent some time prepping my Dad as to where we were going and what we were going to do. I wanted him to know that this was all about him. That everything we were doing was for his benefit. I went slow and tried to get his agreement on the events to come. There would be a Doctor, there would be some questions and if at any time he had a problem all he had to do was let me know. Mom would try and break into my little motivational speech with warm personal phrases like, "don't tell him that" and "you don't know" and "you're scaring him."

The doctor's office was on Upper James Street in a professional building close to the Hospital. We sat down in the waiting room which had been decorated by the same decorating company that decorates all waiting rooms. There were a stack of National Geographic magazines that no one ever touches because you know that everyone who comes into this room is sick. Pamphlets that no one would ever read because that would tell everyone else in the room what was wrong with you. I mean, if you pick up the pamphlet on syphilis everyone knows this is not some light reading. And who in their right mind would take a drink from the fountain or use the washroom. You certainly are not going to use the washroom after the guy who read the leprosy pamphlet went in there before you.

We sit in the corner chairs and Dad let's a rumbling, thunderous fart loose in the room. He pays no attention to the Richter scale moving event. Mom looks up sheepishly at those in the room who do manage to glance into our little conclave, a big mistake on her part, now most of the people in the room are casting ballots in favor of her as the culprit. I sit there shaking in quiet laughter and thinking what a brilliant strategy my Dad has employed to throw the people off the scent, so to speak. Draw attention away from your head where nothing is working and redirect their attention to your ass where everything is working overtime. They finally come for us and as we cross the threshold to the inner sanctum of the Doctor's examining rooms Dad leaves our new friends in the waiting room with another running fart. Money starts to exchange hands amongst the people of the waiting room. An old lady who is paying out most of the cash says, "I could have sworn it was the fat lady."

The Doctor is there to receive us and we all sit around his

small desk and he asks questions of Mom and me trying to piece together a medical history. There is not a lot to tell him. Dad has never had a Doctor, he has never had a need for a Doctor until now. After he appears to have finished his line of questioning I volunteer that his Father had suffered from mental illness at a young age and that he had died at around fifty years of age. Mom blurts out "It was shell shock from the first world war." The Doctor makes a note of my comment.

"What I would like to do now is a little cognitive test with you Glenn. Would that be all right with you?" "Yep." So far Dad is batting a thousand.

Please just answer my questions to the best of your ability. "Who is the Prime Minister of Canada?" Laughingly my Dad answers "Trudeau." "Yes," says the Doctor. I want to ask the doctor if cheering is permitted. "Glenn, what year is it?" Dad just sits there looking at the Doctor. I thought it was trick question. "Glenn, do you know what year it is?"

"Nope." Somewhere in my mind Bob Barker is pushing a brand new car back behind a stage curtain. "Glenn, do you know what day it is?"

"Nope." Oh, ask him his favorite color. A few more questions and the game is over. He doesn't know why he is here and where here is. The Doctor asks us to wait in the outer room while he gives my Father a physical. We sit down in the corner seats again which oddly enough are the only chairs available. Mom says, "He was really close on some of those answers." I sit there and contemplate the possibilities on whether the Doctor would consider keeping my Mother and I'll take my Dad.

The Doctor calls us back into his office and tells us "There is definitely a mental disorder of some kind, probably a dementia that your Father is suffering from. I have referred him to a specialist for further testing. The specialist's office will be in touch with you."

We all climb into the front seat of the Pontiac. I don't know why they both want to sit in the front seat with me. I'm the only one of the three of us who can drive and with us all jammed into that front seat that becomes questionable. Mom illuminates the dark mood in the car with "I was hoping they could give him a pill and he would snap out of it." I think to myself that I wouldn't mind one of those pills right about now.

AND I SIT DOWN NOW TO REST, LOVE, WITH THEE,
EVERY STAR THAT STUDS THE SKY,
SEEMS TO STAND AND WONDER WHY,
THEY'RE SO DIMMER THAN YOUR EYE, SWEET MARIE.

Now, with Dad staying at home and Mom assuming the role of principle care giver, I no longer have the responsibility of having to take Dad to work at five o'clock in the morning and pick him up at six o'clock in the evening. I foolishly believe that this changing of the guard, so to speak, will relieve me of some of the burden of having to take care of my Father.

I quickly realize this responsibility that has supposedly been assumed by my Mother is just an opportunity to add more lyrics to her heart breaking ballad, Oh Poor Me!

Like every other challenge and difficulty she has encountered throughout her life she buries her head in the sand and refuses to attend to the situation rather than develop solutions and strategies to deal with problem.

My Father is going to have to be given routines. Regular meals will need to be provided. Supervised activities. Attention to regular hygiene, bathing and toileting. Measures must be put in place to prevent him from injuring himself and others. My Mom takes the bull by the horns and calls Doctor Dye and asks, "What alcohol can he have?" The Doctor responds with a medical flare and says, "Don't give him rye that will only make him drowsy. Give him brandy, that's a stimulant." The depth of my Mother's understanding of the problems knows no bounds.

Mom does nothing to focus on the reality of the situation and soon I am informed of many of my Fathers sojourns into the community. He is making quite a name for himself as a frequent visitor to neighbors and businesses in the surrounding local.

There are not any wanted posters or warrants out him yet but give him time.

A neighbor around the other side of the block informs me, "Your Father stopped by the other day." That's interesting. My Dad had never been to there house before. Their son and I were friends when we were growing up. We probably hadn't seen each other in five years. "Oh" as nonchalant as possible, "what did he want?"

"A beer. It was eight o'clock in the morning." I couldn't think of anything to come back with so I said, "did you give him one?"

"Yes, he sat at our kitchen table and drank a beer and then left." I explained the situation as best as I could. I asked the neighbor that if my Dad should make an appearance again directing him home would be much appreciated. What was weird about that episode is my Dad did not drink beer.

Word would filter through to me of various sightings of my Father visiting with people he didn't know or just wandering through the neighborhood streets with his khaki garden pants and Italian underwear top. Informing my Mother of these little excursions was a complete waste of time and usually ended badly. She would fall back on her usual pat sentences, "I can't be everywhere at once, I need eyes in the back of my head to keep track of your Father."

"Try getting out of bed before three o'clock." And the fight would be on. The fight always ended the same way. It didn't matter who was sparing in the word ring with her, Julie or me, the fight always ended the same way, "You kids never appreciate anything I do around here."

"That's because you don't do anything around here." The back door would slam until the next bout began. And there was always a next bout.

I ran a tab at the local convenience store on behalf of my Father. It was either set up this line of credit with the store or have my Father sent to jail for theft. He had garnered a bit of a reputation as an outlaw. He had fallen in love with Sweet Marie. In order to taste of Sweet Marie's charms he would rush into the store, make a bee line for the chocolate bars and grab a Sweet

Marie, then back out of the store where he would quickly undress her and stuff her into his mouth. He didn't wear a mask, just some nougat and peanuts on his Italian underwear and tell tale smudges of chocolate around the corners of his mouth. Sometimes he would raid the convenience store as often as three times a day. I had a friend who witnessed one of these daring kidnapping events. He said he could see my Father lurking outside of the store door waiting for the perfect opportunity to rush old lady Wheeler's candy counter. He bolted through the door. She had seen him out of the corner of her eye coming in. She made her defensive lunge to the candy counter but he was just too quick for her. My friend paid for the chocolate bar on behalf of my Father. I now understood why many of my friends would come up to me and ask me for thirty five cents. They never wanted to embarrass me they just said that I owed them thirty five cents. I went to Wheeler's Convenience Store and explained the circumstances of my Fathers behavior. I suggested to Mrs. Wheeler that she keep track of anything my Dad might lift from the store and I would be good for it. I was the only kid in the neighborhood who had a credit account with the local convenience store.

It was a real heart to heart with my Dad, "You can't keep stealing things from the store and you could get into serious trouble. There are people out there who wouldn't understand your behavior."

"Yep."

"Now you listen to me, if you want a chocolate bar just go to Mrs. Wheeler and ask for one. I have had a talk with her and she understands the situation. You got that?" "Yep."

A little while later I was in the convenience store to settle up with Mrs. Wheeler on my Dad's account and asked her if everything was okay now. "Your Dad still keeps running in and taking what he wants. I think he thinks it tastes better. Ah hell, it's a bit of exercise for me."

* * *

There is no such thing as justice. I don't care what you call it, fairness, impartiality, righteousness, even handedness or fair dealing. No truth to the saying; he'll get whats coming to him, or; as ye sow, so shall ye reap and I've never seen anybody get their just desserts. Look around and you will see example after example of the lazy people getting rich because some rich aunt left them a pile of money. The early bird only gets eaten by the neighbor's cat. Let's all face the facts that seldom are people paid back for their stupid and lazy actions that are designed to take advantage of the less fortunate.

"What the hell is going on? Why are you ragging on Dad?" My mother was visibly upset when I walked through the door but as soon as she spotted me she seemed to withdraw. "It's nothing." she said. "I sent your Father to the store and he came home with the wrong thing. That's all."

"Well it sure didn't sound like nothing when I came in. What did you ask him to get?"

"It doesn't matter now, forget it." Something wasn't ringing true. Mom wouldn't back down from an altercation like this unless she was trying to pull some stunt and it had backfired. "C'mon, what's up?"

"I sent your Father to the pharmacy to get something for me and he came home with the wrong item."

"Why would you send Dad to pick up a prescription from the drugstore? It's across a busy street, it's a store he is unfamiliar with and the picking up of a prescription is a little too important an errand to entrust to Dad. What are you nuts?" I was angry and yelling at her now. "For your information it wasn't a prescription, it was Kotex pads, smart ass." Now I'm pissed, "You sent Dad too get some Kotex pads for you? If Dad were of sound mind you would never had asked him to do that. You did that out of sheer laziness. Kotex pads; you must be crazy." I am pretty well worn out from this conversation, "So what did he bring home?"

"Popcorn."

So maybe there is justice in the world. "Well I hope its absorbent popcorn."

* * *

It was always nice to imagine that somewhere in the tangled mess of synapses and amyloid protein build up of Dad's brain, my Father was still concocting little surprises which he would spring on my Mother in order to drive her nuts. Of course it wasn't possible but it was sure fun to pretend.

My Father had always kept a spare set of keys to the car up on the door framing in my parents' bedroom closet. I think in all that time he had occasion to use them once when my Brother locked the keys in the trunk. Otherwise they sat on the door framing ledge for as long as he would own that car. When he got a new car the keys would be replaced on the ledge for safekeeping. When we took the keys away from Dad for his safety and the safety of every other driver in a fifty mile radius of him no one remembered the keys on the ledge in the bedroom closet. Five or six years would have gone by and Dad would have been sick for at least three of them.

No one else in the family knew how to drive so when I came home and found the car not in the same spot that I had left it in I was a little surprised. In fact it wasn't parked at all. There was a garbage can that was flattened and jammed under the front of the car, it had obviously been run over. The front of the car was making an attempt at transplanting a Forsythia tree that was at the end of the driveway forming a natural barrier.

This one is a mystery to me, I have the only set of keys to the car. Into the house I go looking for a satisfactory explanation to this conundrum. There at the kitchen table sits Mom looking rather haggard. She looks like a scene from an old western movie where the woman stands by her burnt out wagon after just barely beating off an attack of wild Indians. Even before I ask for an account, I need to savor the scene before me. I know it's not nice of me but I can't help myself. I know, I'm rotten, but fuck it.

"You look like you have been through the wringer," I try and act cool but the anticipation is killing me. "Why is the car eating the Forsythia?" I just couldn't keep a lid on my curiosity. "Your Father found the spare set of keys on the ledge in the closet."

"Holy shit! How in hell did he ever remember that those keys were there? So did you guys go out for a little spin this afternoon?" A lampoon here, a lampoon there. "Don't be an ass, he tried to run me down."

"Looks like he did." I get that look that only mothers can give. That look that says if I could put you back where you came from I would. She takes both hands and pulls the skin back along both sides of her face, a temporary face lift, and begins her tale.

"I heard the car start in the driveway. I thought maybe you had skipped school and were going to goof off this afternoon. I was on the back porch hanging out some wet things on the line. I came around the side of the house and it was your Father sitting behind the wheel. I started forward towards the car and he put the car in forward and came after me. I put my hands on the hood and held the car back from running over me." In my head are the pictures of what she is saying. First, the driveway is so narrow that you can't go after anyone, you can go forward or you can go backward. Secondly, that Pontiac had a flat head, six cylinder engine that developed one hundred and sixty seven horsepower, you couldn't hold it back. But I'm enjoying the telling of the story so I don't interrupt her. "He kept coming after me so I put the garbage can in front of the car to try and stop him. He just drove over it. I got between the Forsythia and the car and he kept coming forward. I had to squeeze myself out from between the car and the Forsythia tree." Third, a galvanized garbage can is not going to stop a Pontiac sedan, as evidenced of the garbage can that now lay flattened under the car in the driveway. Fourth, mice squeeze, three hundred pound people pop out, cause if they don't they get squished. "So where's Dad now?"

"He is sleeping in his chair in the living room. I think he wore himself out trying to kill me this afternoon."

"I don't think he was trying to kill you."

"You didn't see the look on his face." I may have not seen the look on his face that afternoon but I didn't need to, I had experienced it myself, a few times.

* * *

Like a scene out of a grade B horror movie he approached her with his arms out stretched. His hands and fingers grabbing and clutching in a motion that told her he was going for her throat. He was completely naked except for the gloves he wore. He stumbled forward, as he rocked from side to side, shifting his weight from one naked leg to the other. And always the gloved hands came toward her. Those horrible, hideous gloved hands, red, satin, evening, full length evening gloves.

Dad had been going through Mom's drawers and for some reason, a reason that was known only to him. He figured it was necessary to take off all his clothes and in a motion reminiscent of a bad "B" horror movie, come out of the bedroom, clad only in the red satin evening gloves. I wished I had been there to see that!

Of course when Mom was telling me about it later that evening see added all the dramatics, "Do you think he was going to try and strangle me?"

"Don't know, how did you get him to stop?"

"I was in the kitchen at the sink and when I turned around he was coming at me and I screamed. He just turned around and went back into the bedroom. I checked on him a little later and he was having a snooze. What do you think he was doing?" she asked. "I don't know, maybe he was just having a bit of fun at your expense", but I wish I had been there to see that!

* * *

It was Good Friday and a beautiful spring day, warm and sunny. Elizabeth was in her room preparing to attend the Good Friday services at Saint John's. She skipped off to church wearing a spring type frock and I remember thinking how pretty she looked. Inwardly I wished her well and hoped her attendance at church would provide her with an uplifting and comforting experience. Those feelings of comfort derived from going to church had departed a while ago for me. I was involved in a pickup game of baseball at a local ball field. It was a great day and a good afternoon for baseball.

I got home from the game and was getting a glass of water from the kitchen sink when mom came by and matter of factly told me that my sister was up in her room crying. Her depth of concern for her daughter's tears could have been measured in millimeters. What could have happened to spoil her afternoon? I went to investigate.

Her bedroom door was closed but through the door I could hear her sobbing. I knocked lightly and entered. She was face down on her bed. She still had on the spring dress but it didn't look nearly as pretty as it had just a few short hours ago.

She was weeping as I had never heard anyone weep before. I asked her if she was hurt or in pain and couldn't imagine what could cause such hurt.

She managed to whimper that she wasn't injured. I put my hand on the small of her back and softly asked "Well what's the matter? I saw you just a few hours ago looking very pretty and you looked happy. What's happened?" With my hand on her back I could feel her wracking sobs. I would make an attempt at getting her to confide in me and she would cry all the more. I was getting concerned for her heart. If this was how they broke she was well on her way. "Come on now, you have got to tell me what's wrong so I can help you." Through sobs and faltering words she began. "I had gone to church and was sitting in church," and she would bawl and gulp air in between sobs. "I was in my pew when all of a sudden Dad was standing there looking at me." I was wondering if she was seeing an apparition, maybe a hallucination. Why would Dad be standing in the church? "Help me out here, Dad was standing in the church?" "Yea!" a yowl sound came from Elizabeth. "He was wearing those old shorts and his Italian underwear shirt. I got out of my pew and went to him. I took him by the hand and brought him home." Loud sobbing and an imploring question not directed to anyone but put out there to the universe, "Why would he do that to me?"

It was hard to fathom the embarrassment a twelve year old girl would have suffered while an entire church full of her friends and neighbors would have looked on. I was in tears myself. Not because of her embarrassment but because at that moment I was so proud of the courage she had shown by taking her Father's hand and leading him passed those who would gawk and snicker. It would have taken great spiritual strength for Elizabeth to have walked her Father out of the church.

I needed to help her understand that there was a reason that this happened. That there was something that she could take from this experience that was good. That she has honor and that she has love. Love, that was it.

I got her to sit up and look at me. "What I have to say is important."

"Ah you're just going to tell me some bull."

"No I'm not. I'm going to tell you the truth. Dad went looking for you because he loves you very much."

"Oh, that's a load of crap."

"It is not. It's the truth. Dad has always had a special place in his heart for you. You know that better than anybody. You could always get me into trouble just crying and pointing at me. Dad would come over and cuff me even if there wasn't a reason."

Finally I get a little smile out of her, we are on the road to recovery. "You weren't around and he just wanted to make sure his little girl was all right, granted he could have picked a better time and place." I get another little smile. "I think what you did, how you stood up in a church full of people and walked out, hand in hand, is the bravest thing I have heard of. And if that don't prove that you two love each other... well I don't know what would."

A little later Elizabeth comes down from her bedroom. She's dressed in her play clothes and announces she is going off to her friend's house. She passes by me and says "Thanks John." And she passes by my Father and gives him a kiss on the cheek. It makes me smile. Mom takes notice of the exchange and as if a contended moment were illegal in this house looks at me and says, "Aren't you the little hero."

"Yep," says my Dad.

SERVITUDE

The weekly disability pay, if we can give it a civil name, was suppose to be picked up every Saturday night at the fish stores closing time, six o'clock.

Mom would start nagging around two in the afternoon to make sure that I would not be late for the pickup. "Now be sure and get there on time. If you're not there they will leave and we won't have any money for the week. Are you listening to me?"

"I'll be sure to be there on time. I'll catch them before they leave. You'll have your money for the week. Don't worry."

I hated this time of the week. When I would turn up at the store they would make me stand in the back of the store. They being Junior and Cybil. Cybil was Junior's wife. I suppose that made her my aunt but I tried not to think about her in those terms. She was a short plump woman. She wasn't what you would call fat but everywhere you looked she was round. She didn't have a waist so with large tits and a large bum and no waist she resembled the numeral eight, she was just two circles with a head on top.

My mother disliked here immensely. She said that when Junior had first started to date her they all thought she was retarded because she was always playing with dolls. I think the real reason she didn't get on with her was that Junior and her lived in Bernia's big house off the Lakeshore. Without having to pay for a mortgage they would have had a greater amount of disposable income to spend on the things that Cybil liked to spend money on, and that was decorating. She wasn't particularly good at it, she just couldn't leave anything alone. Cybil was fond of gold accents. Every valance, window frame and door frame had some swirling cheap looking gold accent painted on. It made you want to duck your head when passing through the portal.

Junior and Cybil had one child to attest to the consummation of their marriage. After that time she decided she didn't like it but it was too late she was pregnant and gave birth to a son. Of course nobody liked him. It wasn't his fault. He was spoiled rotten. He was given piano lessons, golf lessons, hockey lessons, his bedroom looked like the Smithsonian Institute.

It was a family tradition, tradition is the wrong word. It was a family chore that every Christmas was spent at Junior and Cybil's. Bernia and Percival would have made the drive up from Florida, Cybil would invite all her relatives and the two families that had absolutely nothing in common and had not spoken since the Christmas before came together to work through an afternoon of too much booze, dry turkey and Christmas pudding with a rum sauce that was capable of stripping paint. My cousin would be showcased at his organ and would play his entire repertoire which consisted of the Marine's Halls of Montezuma and then, because everyone enjoyed hearing him play, Cybil would ask him to play it again.

After my cousins' recital ended Cybil's twin brothers would start up. One of them played the organ and was an entertainer in a bar downtown. Some dive that could advertise Live Entertainment as a drawing card. The other brother was the one that helped Cybil paint the fake gold leaf on everything. Certainly no limit to the talent in her family. I didn't know which brother was which and I didn't care. The one who played the organ would sing Hello dolly and going around the room would replace dolly with Olivia, Cybil, June, Betty, ad nausea.

The evening would end as it always ended. The kids would pile into the frozen backseat of the Pontiac and begin to shiver with the cold. Mom would bitch to Dad all the way home, "I can't stand going there year after year. Why can't we skip it next year? I can't stand Cybil's family. She painted the living room again, did you notice?" Dad would ignore her. The following Christmas we would be back.

So here I was standing at the back of the store watching the two of them preparing to close the store. They seemed to be making an extra effort to show me how hard they were working. They were working at working at it. Cybil was the best at it. She would grunt and groan while wiping down the freezer cases, glancing over to me to see if I was aware of her obvious struggles and painful exertions. What had caught my eye was the way she looked. She wore a print house dress, gaudy red flowers on a white background. Over the dress, what once was probably a nice cranberry colored knit cardigan sweater was now stretched and pulled so that the wool had spaces that resembled a gill net. On top of that she wore a white butcher's jacket. Her hair was in a netting of some kind. She had probably started out the day in nylon stockings, the kind that hook up to a girdle. Sometime during the day she had decided that this was way too uncomfortable and unhooked the nylons. She had rolled them neatly down her legs to the tops of her shoes. She looked like she had foreskins around her ankles.

They continued with their game of making me wait and trying to make me feel uncomfortable, I was doing my best to look upbeat and positive. There was no way in hell I was going to let them think they were getting to me. Cybil was acting out the part, brushing past me in a great hurry to get to nowhere. "Anything I can do for you?" I asked with the most cheerful nuance I could gather. "You just stand there and wait until your uncle and I have finished all our work." She could not have been more unkind in her tone of voice. She was itching for a fight. I was more determined than ever not to give it to her. She couldn't control herself any longer. Cybil took the envelope from the pocket of her white butcher's jacket. She grabbed me by my coat and put her face so close to mine that I could easily watch the individual veins that were exploding and erupting in the whites of her eyes.

She drove the envelope into my chest and hissed, "This is blood money!"

She let go of me and dropped the envelope on purpose. She wanted to see me picking the envelope and the money it contained from the floor. Her idea of humiliating me further in this situation. She wanted to see me grovel. Employing every ounce of self restraint I bent over and scooped the envelope from the floor with one sweeping motion. I placed it on the inside of my jacket, I didn't even have a pocket there but I thought it looked dramatic. "Good evening, I hope you have a grand weekend." I stepped to the back door and opened it neither too fast nor too slow. I stepped confidently through the door which I closed behind me. I walked at a normal pace to the car and drove around the corner, past the front of the store and yelled, "Fuck you!" It was totally for my benefit. "Fuck You!" It's amazing how good you can feel shouting at the top of your lungs in a car all by yourself.

When I got home I gave the envelope to my mother, "Any problems?" she asked. "No, they were as nice as pie."

* * *

When Mom was negotiating with Junior for her weekly stipend I didn't realize that she was using me as a bargaining chip. She told Junior that I would be available to work in the store, gratis, any time he needed me. I suppose selling your children's services has been going on since the dawn of man however, just like being run over by a garbage truck, you don't think it's going to happen to you until it happens to you.

Junior and Cybil must have felt that they didn't get a big enough chunk of my ass because they were on the phone to my mother asking that I work at the fish store every Saturday from now until Christmas and all during the holiday school break. When Mom informed me of my anticipated schedule I was appalled at the prospect. When she told me that she had offered my services to them as part of the money negotiation and that I wasn't to be paid anything, I was apoplectic. I had never told her what went on when I picked up the money each Saturday night, not that it would have made a difference. I'm sure that as long as she was getting her money she wouldn't have given a shit at what I had to suffer in order to get it. I just knew after our last

111

encounter that Junior and Cybil wanted another piece of me. "By the way," I asked as off handed as I could possibly sound under the circumstances, "who called, Junior or Cybil?" "It was Cybil."

"Fucking bitch," I said not quite under my breath. "What was that?"

"Nothing", old habits die hard.

The next Saturday I had put on my long underwear, flannel lined jeans and snowmobile boots. I was way ahead of those jerks when it came to dressing for freezing temperatures. I grabbed one of Dad's old white shirts and a tie from his closet and put this shirt and tie on over all my warm clothes. I couldn't resist the idea that they would be thinking I was under dressed for the long cold day ahead. I had planned that when I got to the store I would wear only a white butcher's jacket over all my nice warm clothes.

I arrived at the store and entered through the back door. I moved confidently through to the office where I hung up my winter jacket and put on a white jacket. I noticed that Cybil had added some accoutrements to the office. There was a hot plate and a kettle and a tea pot sitting on top of the old safe. The shot glasses still sat on the inside window ledges. "Good morning, what can I do?"

"Get out to the freezer and start bringing in the trays for the freezer cases." No good morning, no please, just get out to the freezer."

"No problem." I would bring in all the trays loaded with their different product and hand them over to Junior and Cybil as they waited for me to deliver them. I can see that this was going to be a real slug fest. They are going to use me as a gopher for every little thing that they could get away with. Fortunately I am not familiar enough with the counter and the cash or they would have probably left me here alone for the day.

Cybil goes into the office and sets the kettle to boiling and Junior pours his first shot of the day, it's seven thirty in the morning. "Breakfast of champions." I say to him. He scowls and knocks it back. I notice as Cybil is sitting down to enjoy her tea that she is wearing the same outfit she had on last Saturday complete with the foreskin ankles. I figure she must pull them up when she goes home just in case the fashion police are in her driveway; wouldn't want to be caught improperly attired, however, smelling like a mackerel is perfectly acceptable.

Junior wants me to scale some fish that are in a tub, "You remember how to scale a fish don't you?"

"Yes I remember how to scale a fish. Where are they?" I remember last time I was assigned this task. That day I scaled something like two tons of fish. It was boring work, but if that's what will get them off my back, fine. "Where are they?"

"Out back." I don't remember seeing the great white tubs when I came in and I didn't think there had been a delivery since I got here. I go out back and through the alley but I can't see the fish. Back I go into the store. The last thing I want to do is speak with these assholes. "Excuse me Junior, I can't seem to see the fish in the alley anywhere." Cybil comes charging out of the office, "He is your Uncle Junior, show some respect," she snaps. She has been waiting for some reason to go on the offense and she figures this may be her best opportunity. I ignore her and look to Junior for direction. "They're not in the alley they're in the freezer. There are four twenty five pounder cases." One hundred pounds of fish to scale, that's child's play. Then it dawns on me. They don't have the wholesale side of the business anymore. Without my Dad to run that side of things they have gone to retail only. They might as well have a fish cart in the street. I go back out to the freezer and take a closer look at things. The freezer is empty compared to what it was when they were wholesalers. Most of the product they now received came in twenty or forty pound cases. A lot of it was frozen. The sole and other mainstays were in fresh plastic tubs but in much smaller quantities. The variety was certainly less. The exotics are gone.

I am merrily about my work when around eight o'clock Pots reports for work. We greet each other like old friends, "It's good to see you. How are things going?" I am truly happy to see anyone who can smile and speak without venom dripping from their lips. Pots is the last of the truck drivers. The store once employed as many as five drivers. Now, it only took one gink to easily handle the errands of picking up the fish from wholesalers and making a run to the liquor store. "How long are you going to be working here?" Pots asks. "Until those assholes hear about the Emancipation Proclamation," I say in a low tone. "Until when?"

"Forget it." I say. "Well it's good to see you anyway, hey Pans, how's your Dad?" That's enough socializing for Cybil, she assigns Pots some mundane task, she doesn't want the source of the blood money discussed in any context what so ever.

The day passes slowly. I finish up the scaling and move on to checking for parasites in the sole fillets. There isn't enough work to keep four persons busy all day. As the day drags on Junior gets into his cups. Cybil gets colder and nastier until she has worked herself into frenzy. She is now looking for a fight. She needs to vent. She needs to be able to pick on someone who is not going to be able to fight back. She feels that if she can piss me off I'll walk and they won't have to pay the weekly stipend to my Father. She begins her tirade with jabs about her having to work in the store because my Father is lazy. "He's only pretending to be sick so he can loaf around." Cleaning one of the freezer showcases as she directs her rant to a tray of trout that oblige her by obediently staring back at her. She continues, "Your Father took all that money and is hiding it somewhere. He stole it, he is a lazy and shiftless man." I look to Junior to see if he is going to make any kind of effort to stifle his bitch. Like a dog who has just shit on the carpet he skulks away to the front of the store and pretends to be looking out the window. In order to engage Junior in the conversation and to try and put an end to her attack I ask Junior, "is there anything else I can do or is that about it?" Junior, the weakling looks at Cybil, she stops him in his tracks with a look. And she starts in again, "you just want to get your hands on that blood money don't you?" I step to the back of the store. I want to put some distance between me and Cybil. Pots is in the back of the store and has been listening to the entire poisonous conversation. "Why don't you tell the bitch to fuckoff," he says. "I need that money for my family, it's my Dad's money and we have a right to it." I am pretty close to tears, struggling to keep control of my emotions. Pots' says "Well I was looking for a job when I found this one." He walks up to Cybil and asks for his pay envelope. She grudgingly reaches in to the till and gives him his money. "You are a fucking bitch,"he says "and you," looking at Junior, "are a gutless cocksucker." He drops his coveralls where he is standing and leaves the store. He crosses Cannon Street to the parking lot and gets into the City Fish pickup truck and starts the engine. He doesn't go anywhere. He revs the engine until he blows the head gasket off the top of the engine, then he leaves. Meanwhile.

"Now see what you have done. You have made us lose our driver."

"Can I have my Dad's money, please?" Flustered and losing the muscle of her arguments, she gives me the envelope. I stuff the envelope into my back pants pocket, the appropriate repository for City Fish capital, and step through the back door. I hesitate, pop my head back in and say, "The reason you lost your driver is because you Aunty Cybil, are a fucking bitch and you Uncle Junior, are a gutless cocksucker."

When I get into the house there is Mom in the kitchen doing her tap, tap, tap with her toe on the tile. She looks like a refrigerator auditioning for the Rockettes. "I just got off the phone with your aunt Cybil."

"I'm not surprised," I said. "She said that you swore and cussed them."

"That would be correct."

"She said you're not allowed to set foot in that store again and that if I want the weekly money that I have to go up there myself and get it. Well I'll tell you that you're going to drive me up there and wait in the car until I have finished my business."

"Why I'd be happy to drive you." I wouldn't miss this for the world.

Saturday arrives and Mom is ready to go at five o'clock. I tell her that they would prefer you come closer to six. "Oh, I'll just pop into the store and get the money and be back out in a jiff." When we are getting closer to the store I am heading for the corner parking lot. Mom says, "Just pull up and let me out in front of the store and I'll just be a second." "I think I'll park in the parking lot if you don't mind."

"I don't know why you're going to make me walk all the way to the store from the parking lot?"

"Mom, it's just across the street." She gets out of the car in a huff and stomps off to the store. It is five twenty in the afternoon.

It is now six fifteen in the evening. My first glimpse of her is as she is crossing Cannon Street at the light. I would not have believed it was possible that she was capable of such velocity. She was traveling at a dangerous speed. Her bulk and speed were combining to create a hazardous vortex. Fortunately she was the only person in the crosswalk as the turbulence could have easily thrown an innocent pedestrian into traffic. She stomps up to the car, opens the door and lands on the passenger's seat with such force that the car rocked noticeably to the right. She is livid. "Do you know what those people said to me?" Without waiting for me to answer, "They said it was blood money. They said you Father was pretending to be sick." She was starting to bawl. "They called him a thief." I looked at her and put my hand on her shoulder and said, "I know, they say that every time I come up here to get our pay and they say those things all day long while I'm working here." She looked at me with a heavy sadness in her eyes, "I didn't know."

"Would it have made a difference to you if I had told you?" She sat quietly for the rest of trip home. We would continue picking up the money and taking their abuse, but we both knew something had to change.

MACASSA

Mom had a million "what would happen to me if" scenarios that she would play out whenever the paranoia in the Seagrams hit. Back on those Sundays when she and dad would be sitting at the kitchen table drinking, from somewhere in some dusty corner of her mind would come the question, what would happen if? And she had a lot of them. During the Cuban missile crisis she had a, "What if you were at work and an air raid took place. I can't see me dragging mattresses down the cellar steps for protection for the kids and me against a nuclear explosion." I don't think my Dad had an answer to that one except maybe, "How about another drink?"

"What would happen if something were to happen to you? How would me and the kids live? What would we do for money? We would lose the house. I'd have to take a typing course."

"The store would take care of you," he would say. "You don't have to worry about a thing, we have a business agreement."

"Well I don't think an agreement between you and Junior will help me out." Dad didn't like these conversations. In all of the scenarios he was dead. "It's not a verbal agreement, it's a partnership agreement, and it's between Ma and Junior and me. It lays out what happens to our shares in the event of one of our deaths or sickness. You'll be well taken care of."

Dad always believed that because that was the kind of guy he was. He took care of my Grandma when Gramps died and he would have taken care of Junior if something had of happened to him, agreement or no agreement. That's just the way he was built.

* * *

Emil and Alois, sound like the German equivalent of Amos and Andy. They could easily be mistaken for a vaudeville routine or an early radio program. Not! These two guys were the co-discoverers of the disease named after Alois. They worked alongside of each other in Emil Kraepelin's laboratory. In 1906 the neuropathology was first observed by Alois. Emil agreed that the disease should bear the name of his colleague, Alzheimer's.

Dad would be diagnosed with a rare form of Alzheimer's, EOFAD, or Early Onset Familial Alzheimer's Disease. Of the seventy two types of dementia, Alzheimer's is the most common. Only four to five percent of all Alzheimer's is of the early onset type. It strikes at the ages of fifty to sixty years and the familial is usually far more aggressive in nature.

The disease is inherited in an autosomul dominant fashion. That means that only one parent passes the gene. It also means that should that carrier produce four offspring then there is a fifty percent chance that two of the children could inherit the gene. If the other two do not develop the disease then they will not pass it on.

Early Onset Familial Alzheimer's Disease is invariably fatal. As the disease claims more of the brain the patient loses the ability to perform complex tasks such as driving and money management. In the latter stages of the disease simple hygiene becomes beyond their ability and full time care is required. Although people do not die directly from the disease, as the bodies systems begin to shut down other complications take over, such as pneumonia, resulting in death.

* * *

Now that we had a firm diagnosis in hand and the prospects for any kind of recovery defunct, it was time to think about the family's future.

The partnership agreement was a good place to start. Now that it was confirmed that Dad would not be returning as an active partner to the store we should secure what was legally ours. As Dad had always claimed, the store will take care of you. It was time to see exactly what the store was prepared to take care of.

Mom decided to seek the council of a school friend of my brothers who was now a lawyer. I didn't think that using a friend was such a good idea. I knew this guy and a law degree certainly wasn't going to increase the value of his stock in my opinion. Mom thought he would be clever and cheap. He was neither.

With her copy of the City Fish and Poultry Ltd. partnership agreement firmly in hand she went off to her meeting with her new legal advisor. I didn't see her until later that day and when I did catch up with her besides meeting with her lawyer see had obviously been visiting with the Seagrams. Mom's eyes were red and her tongue was rather thick. I did not want to go where she had gone. "How did the meeting go with your lawyer?"

"Horrible!" The word sounded like it had too many R's in it. "What happened?"

"He said that I didn't have a leg to stand on." She bent down to her purse that was beside the kitchen table. She took a couple of swipes at the handles, missed them both times. I lifted her hand bag on to the table, she began to rifle through her bag and produced an envelope that was somewhat crushed and scrunched. She took a piece of lined paper from the envelope that had been written on in pencil, "I wrote down exactly what he said." Mr. Seagram's had taken a toll on her tongue. She was speaking as though her mouth was filled with feathers. She held out the paper with both hands. I watched her as she tried to focus on the written words. She wasn't making it easy on herself. The paper she was holding was moving in circles because her arms kept moving. Her head was slowly rocking from side to side in a delayed action as she couldn't keep up to the swirling paper and her eyes rolled about quite independently of one another. "Let me read this for you, *there is a clause that precludes any attempt for an action on our part with regards to recovery of remuneration concerning City Fish and Poultry Ltd. The clause states clearly that should any of the partners suffer a mental illness of any kind, they shall forfeit his or her shares to the remaining partners.*" I sat there stunned. Literally amazed at what I had read.

It took a while to totally comprehend the implications of this clause inserted into a business agreement by a mother against her boys.

Against is the correct word. A clause that had been inserted for the sole purpose of robbing one of her boys. Of denying one of her offspring his right to his legacy. Bernia knew what she was doing. She must have begun to formulate this plan back when she was locking her husband away in the store cellar. And Junior would have known about the clause when he was locking his brother away in the cellar as his mother had done to his father. She knew her husband was not suffering from shell shock. She must have had some discussions with doctors who would have informed her about the disease and the fact that the disease could be passed on to the sons. After all, the disease had been discovered over forty years before.

Could it have been possible that at some time Junior would have informed his mother that Glenn was slipping? That he wasn't quite doing his share at the store. Would Bernia, not knowing the depth of the financial seriousness that the store was sinking into, told her eldest son not to worry? Knowing about the clause in the agreement she was prepared to let it ride until such time as she could trigger the clause in the agreement and capture Glenn's shares. Junior, who through laziness or just plain stupidity, was not aware of the state of affairs and would have done what his mother said, nothing.

Not until it was too late, would they discover their greed had back fired on them. That Glenn was quietly driving them into bankruptcy.

No wonder that they thought Dad was stealing from them. They were already thinking along those lines. They were going to legally steal from Dad through the clause in the agreement. They must have thought that Dad had beaten them to it. Now everything they had was worthless. At fifty years old Junior was going to become a retail fish monger. Bernia, who had retired by the sweat of her boys, was going to take a huge cut in pension funds. Percival got a job painting houses. Cybil stopped painting gold leaf accents in her house and went to work in the fish store alongside her husband.

Why, in a person's greatest time of need, when they are most vulnerable and need love and support, would the person most capable of providing for the needs, protecting their vulnerabilities, supporting and loving the afflicted person, plan to destroy them. Most people wouldn't do that to a stranger. I could not imagine what kind of mother would do it to her son.

* * *

Dad's illness was taking its toll on him and everyone around him. He was in free fall mentally. Dad required twenty four hour care and even that, at times was not enough. My mother had never been attentive to her children and now she was trying to control a one hundred and ninety pound kid. Dad still had a lot of physical strength so preventing him from doing something once he got it into his head could be difficult and at times, even dangerous. Dad and I still had some kind of understanding.

It is hard to explain but most of our communication was done through the eyes. I could see in his eyes moments of lucidness. I would be trying to get him to do something like stopping him from eating an entire box of corn flakes. I would tell him to stop but that would get little response. If I could look at him directly in the eye and say, "No more, you have to stop now." Somewhere inside his head connections would link up and he would understand. His eyes would tell me that there had been a coherence of some kind. On other occasions the eyes were dull and lifeless. I was always on the lookout for those brief periods of cognitive behavior. To see his eyes comprehending and reacting to what was being said was a real treat for me.

I wondered if he were being held a prisoner by some radical faction inside his mind. If there was a war between the Sanes and the Insanes. Those moments of brightness within his eyes were times when the Sanes had beaten back the Insanes. When they had the upper hand in the land of Glenndor. The Sanes would run to the windows of his eyes and cheer and yell, "We're still here! We are all still here!" Then the Insanes would attack again. The Sanes would have to turn away from the windows and the eyes would fall dim once more. The battles must have been fierce for the Sanes seldom came to the windows of the eyes in the land of Glenndor. And lately it seemed they were coming even less.

* * *

Dad was becoming a danger to himself. He had almost choked himself to death while eating some chicken. It was stupid to give him the chicken with bones in it but somehow it got by us. He was chewing and swallowing the whole leg and of course it got stuck in his throat.

On one occasion in the blink of an eye he had found and was about to eat some moth balls. The smell of the balls gave him away. I wrestled the killer candy away from him in the nick of time.

What we use to be able to find humor in was now a daily struggle to keep ahead of him. He had all day to think up or plan these raids of one kind of another. We had to get him into an institution where he could receive proper care.

Making that major decision is another feeling of failure for the care givers. You know you are losing the battle. Whether it is rational to feel that way is irrelevant. You can't help feeling that it is just another battle lost and a little closer to losing the war.

At the time there were no agencies or support groups. Unfortunately, you were pretty much on your own. Doctors didn't even have any advice for you because there were no facilities for a guy Dad's age with an affliction of his type. Enter, Macassa Lodge.

Macassa Lodge was established in the late 1840's. Originally set up for the treatment of immigrants that would arrive from an

Atlantic crossing sick and diseased. In addition it would care for those too poor and infirmed to take care of themselves. In the early years of its existence it was situated down by the Hamilton Bay. Back then the bay was known by the name Macassa, hence the name. Around 1950 they built a new facility on Hamilton Mountain. In the 1960's it was known as an old folks home.

Somewhere we got a lead and were directed to the Macassa Lodge. It cared for the elderly in an institutional setting. That means it had a fenced in property and controlled entrances and exits. That means that you couldn't get out.

They were sympathetic to our situation but the problem was that my Dad was only fifty years of age. They had never admitted anyone that young. He didn't qualify as he was under the age of admission. It seemed to me that under the age of admission applied to roller coasters and bars. Finally they recanted. Dad became the youngest resident in the Macassa Lodge. The staff referred to him as the youngster.

The building was dated but clean. The mandatory institutional green lino on the floor. The dull grey walls with metal railings covered in thick black plastic ran along each side, there to assist the residents in negotiating the halls. The smell of bleach mixed with the smell of urine. There were old guys who would say Hi to you and old guys who wouldn't say boo. Some guys would turn and face the wall when they saw you coming and some guys looked at you with a big grin happy to see you, anticipating that you were coming to see them. And always the sound of the shuffling slippers on the green floor. Sometimes a tray or a bed pan would hit the floor with a loud clatter. The reaction to this loud crash would cause some of the residents to take shelter from the air raid, others would laugh and clap and stomp their feet feeling that this had been provided for their personal amusement. But most of the time the old guys just sat and stared. Not at anything, right through everything.

I would visit with my Father as often as I could. I didn't want to lose what modest tie was left between us. I could see him going deeper and deeper into himself. He responded to little around him. We would go out to the yard, the staff called it the garden. The garden was securely surrounded by a twenty foot high chain link fence. We would light up a cigarette and Dad would walk right up to the fence and stand there looking out. It was impossible to tell what he might have been thinking as he stared out past the chain link fence. I hoped he was thinking of a young man, who was a dashing pilot in love with a beautiful girl.

Mom would bug me to pick up Dad and bring him down to the house for a visit. She thought it would be a nice change for him. What she didn't realize was that Dad felt secure within the walls of Macassa Lodge. He was familiar with the staff. They provided his food. They provided his clothes and a bed for him. They provided for him and he was completely dependent on them. It was becoming evident that he was uncomfortable when I tried to take him out of this safe and comfortable environment. To ask my mother to understand was almost impossible. She'd say, "Don't be ridiculous, why wouldn't he want to come and visit his home?" The last time I ever took him out of the lodge I had to get one of the orderlies he knew well to help me coax him into the car. When we got to the house he didn't want to sit down. Within fifteen minutes we were back in the car and headed to the lodge. He practically ran through the front doors and down the hall to his room. I refused to take him from, what had become for him, his refuge.

* * *

Henderson General was an older hospital, it had been around since 1917. Back then it was known as the Mount Hamilton Hospital. It served the needs of the World War I veterans. Circa 1950 it became the Henderson General Hospital, a palliative care facility. The chronic care wing was the oldest and dingiest part of the already aged building. Over the doors, at the entrance to the ward, there should have been a great stone lintel with the words carved deep into the stone, "Next Stop?"

Dad was transferred from Macassa Lodge to the chronic ward at Henderson. Like a set of dominoes his systems were shutting down one after the other. His heart, lung and kidneys were all conspiring to sabotage the life force within him. And he had endured the trauma of being dragged out of his sanctuary by strangers in white coats and placed in a strange unfamiliar environment.

What impact would this have had on his mind? Having become so reliant on the Macassa environment, its food, its shelter and the staff who provided for his needs...it must have been a horrific experience. He didn't have the faculties available to ask what was happening to him or why it was happening to him. Everything that he would experience would be cold and scary. Nothing at all would give him the assurance that he would be safe and secure. Everything would lead him to believe the contrary.

Maybe he decided that this was the way it was at the end of one's life. Similar to some Native American and Inuit people's death rites, he was being abandoned to complete his death walk. And so he walked.

The Macassa Lodge notified my Mother that Dad was being transferred to the Henderson. They simply said that he had taken a turn beyond which they were capable of providing for. Mom contacted all her kids and we assembled at the coordinates of the little room in the back end of Henderson Hospital. Dad was hardly conscious, a low rattle came from his throat. As usual in situations of that kind you just sort of look at each other hoping someone has something to say, but nobody ever does.

The vigil continued throughout the day and into the evening. A nurse came into the room and listened to his heart and said "Nothing will happen until the morning. Why don't you go and get some rest. I will be here all night and I will call you if there is any change. Come back early tomorrow morning."

James and Elizabeth went to Julie's and stayed at her place for the night. Mom and I stayed at her sister's which was much closer to the hospital.

I was trying to sleep on the sofa. Mom and her sister and brother in-law were in the kitchen knocking back the Seagrams. I didn't want Mom to get blasted. I didn't need for her to be out of control. She may have been frightened but I knew she would need her wits about her tomorrow. They continued laughing and carrying on loudly into the early morning hour until I finally got up and went into the kitchen. Clearly and plainly I said, "We had better get some sleep now, tomorrow is going to be a big day." Everyone quickly dispersed, like mice scattering because the cat has come into the room.

The phone rang at about five thirty that morning. I rushed over to the phone and lifted the receiver to my ear. "Hello," I said, though my voice sounded as if it were a thousand miles away from me. "This is Henderson General calling regarding a Glenn Duncan?" It was more of a question than a statement. It was as though we had placed an ad in the paper and were selling a Glenn Duncan and Henderson General wanted to know if it was still available. "Yes, go ahead."

"There has been a change in Mr. Duncan's condition. You should come to the hospital as soon as possible."

"Thank you" I said and hung up the phone. I took a deep breath and turned to get my Mother from her room but she was already standing there. "It's time to go," was all I said.

We walked into the room. The room was dimly lit. He lay in his bed propped up a little. His eyes closed. He looked so much smaller than he had just a few hours ago. I walked toward the bed. He coughed, a cracking loud cough and he died.

Mom backed out of the room and sat in a chair that was placed across from the doorway to his room. I could hear James, Julie and Elizabeth coming up the hall way. I went to meet them, tears coursing down my cheeks, my head shaking a despondent no. Mom was holding Elizabeth and saying ""I'm sorry." James and

Julie went into his room to see their Father.

We stood around not knowing what the appropriate time to leave was. We answered some questions as to which funeral home to send the body. No, we wouldn't allow an autopsy for education purposes. Mom collected her two boys together and said we would have to go and buy Dad a new shirt and tie for the viewing. She told us that she planned to have him buried in his gray suit. Finally a nurse came out of her station with a brown paper bag. She stood in the center of us waiting for someone to take the bag. Like idiots, we all just stood there looking at her. Somehow, in the act of accepting the brown paper bag containing the scant effects of Glenn Duncan it was final confirmation of his death. I took the bag and we left.

Elizabeth and Mom went with Julie in her car. James and I left the hospital in my car. We were already, in our minds, with delight, anticipating our tiny shopping errand and how we could have some fun at the expense of some unsuspecting clothing clerk.

It was early Saturday morning and we had to waste a bit of time standing around in front of the men's clothing store waiting for someone to open the doors. I could see a clerk rummaging around in the back of the store so I rapped on the window and motioned for him to let us in. He came to the door and said, "We don't open for another half hour."

"I understand, but we have a special purpose and we would really appreciate it if you would let us in to purchase a shirt and tie."

"Oh, some body's birthday?" he asks. "No, quite the opposite." I replied. "Well, how can I help you?"

"We need a dress shirt," says James. "What size?" asks the clerk? James looks at me and I look at him. The clerk looks at both of us. "He used to be a size sixteen neck but now he is much smaller."

"Been dieting?" asks the clerk. "Sort of," says James. "Let's split the difference and make it fifteen and a half. After all it's not like he is going to be uncomfortable in it."

"What color? Asks the clerk. "Sky blue, what do you think James?"

"Sky blue sounds perfect." The clerk digs through his rack and pulls out the shirt. "This has French cuffs. Does your friend have any cufflinks?"

"He isn't a cufflinks sort of guy. In fact I've never seen him without his sleeves rolled up at any time in his life." James wanders over to the jewelery case. The clerk follows him and lifts the glass display lid. "How about these?" He holds up some gaudy gold cufflinks that look more like chain mail than an elegant accoutrement. "They'll rust," says James. The clerk looks offended, "No they won't!"

"They will where they're going." You can see the clerk beginning to look at us suspiciously. In his mind he is thinking, they don't look drunk. "So, what do you have for ties?" I ask. We all go over to the tie rack and stand around it like kids around a campfire. "As you can see, we have lots of patterns to choose from. What do you think your friend would like."

"Trust me, he won't like anything we pick out for him,"

"Finicky sort is he?"

"Not anymore." The clerk shows me ties with paisley patterns. "Geez, I don't know James, he never wore a paisley tie in his life."

"And he won't wear one in his life now, will he?"

The clerk is reeling. We can see he is having trouble keeping up with the conversation. The clerk rings up all the items and we pay him and he says, "I hope your friend likes his present."

"We're burying a guy in these clothes" says my brother. The clerk, scrambling to come up with something intelligent says, "Have a nice day." As we cross the street on our way back to the car "I wonder how the rest of his day will go." James just laughs and says, "better than ours."

* * *

The family always has a viewing prior to the general visitation.

This is conducted for the express purpose of ironing out any kinks. I knew this because one of my friends worked in his family's funeral home. He was always telling me stories of stuff that went on behind the scenes at a funeral home.

We all went to the funeral home to make the arrangements. I explained to my siblings that the price on the coffin usually included all the peripheral bits and pieces such as the room, the cars and the transportation to the grave side. After that it was the cemetery administrators that handled burial policy.

Upon arriving we were ushered into the Director's office and he laid out the agenda. We entered the show room where the caskets were displayed. Mom wanted to settle on a gray cloth covered casket. "Are you sure that is the one you want?"

"Yes, I'm sure. Let's get that guy in here and tell him we have made a choice."

"You won't have to. He'll come in and walk directly to this casket and ask if you like this one." The director came and walked directly to the grey cloth covered casket and said, "Mrs. Duncan do you like this one?"

The next day was the private family viewing. We all entered the room and stopped at the door. At the end of the room was the casket. From there you could only see his nose above the rim of the casket. I had to actually give myself a mental push to get my legs to carry me across the room to the edge of the casket. After the initial reaction that the guy in the box was really your Father we all noticed that besides sporting a lovely shirt and tie ensemble he also had a rosary threaded through his fingers. "What's he doing with a rosary in his hand? Dad wasn't a catholic." This came out in a choir like unison. I walked over to a plant and spoke into the foliage, "please come and remove the rosary from my Father's hands." The rest of the family must have thought that somewhere in my renunciation of the RC religion I had converted to the Druid faith. Immediately an attendant came into the room, acknowledged the family, pretended he was adjusting a lamp and left the room. When we looked back to my Father the rosary was gone. "How'd you do that?" asked my brother.

Bernia and Percival had made the trip north. We hadn't seen or spoken with them since she had beaten her son on the front porch at Aldous. Junior and Cybil came in with them. Bernia looked at her son in the grey box and said, "Oh, he's gone thin." Percival helped her back to a chair and no one crossed the room to offer condolences to the widow or her family members and too much water had passed under that bridge for me to make the effort.

Tuesday was the burial. There was a final family viewing. We piled into black limousines. We headed for the Holy Sepulcher Cemetery. There was a Police escort that kept the funeral procession all together. They would stop traffic until we had cleared the street, and rush ahead on their motorcycles to the next intersection. Because Dad was a veteran they would stand at attention and salute the hearse as it would pass by.

We gathered at the gravesite where one of the RC priests out of Saint John's parish gave a prayer of thanks for the life of Glenn Duncan. Then with a roar, a squadron, less one, of CF-101 Voodoo, paid honorific respect in a final fly-past. He would have loved that.

We all piled back in to the big black limo. On the way home we asked the chauffeur if he wouldn't mind going by the take out window at the Kentucky Fried Chicken store. He was about to swing in to the KFC when we told him we were just kidding.

AFTERGLENN

Mom needed to go to work. She needed some income. There had been a small ten thousand dollar life insurance policy with the Prudential but the proceeds from that would not last her long. Her dilemma was solved when she ran across a want ad in the local newspaper. Someone was advertising for a housekeeper and daily sitter for a young child.

That somebody was a dentist who had won custody of his child in a divorce and now had to prove to the courts he was able to provide the proper care and wholesome environment. That proper care and wholesome environment came in the person of my Mother. She claimed that the good doctor had asked her what her qualifications were for the job and she had told him that she had raised four children. Wasn't that proof enough of her qualifications? Obviously he was not practicing his due diligence. Had he asked any one of her four children for a reference she may have been turned down flatly for the position.

Her biggest hurdle, after actually securing the placement, was that the house that she was to clean and the kid she was to provide succor to were in Burlington. This forced Mom to have to catch a bus at the downtown terminal every morning.

The Hamilton bus terminal is like every other downtown bus terminal. That's why they are called terminals. Terminal means; fatal, incurable, deadly, mortal, lethal, and life-threatening. This is a perfect description of the people who frequent the bus terminal. Even the word downtown has an ominous resonance to it like; we once had a town but the bus terminal took it down.

Like all bus terminals, this one has a coffee shop. These places are the forerunners of the coffee shops of today that frequent every corner. Back then they didn't call for a coffee latte or a cappuccino. They didn't have grandees they had a fucking cup of coffee. Like all coffee shops this one has its regulars. Mom became one of these regulars. Like all regulars they talk with the other regulars regularly. Enter Jake.

Jake is an appliance salesman for the natural gas company. He likes to hang out at the bus terminal coffee shop across the street from the gas appliance showroom. Jake is a diabetic who pays little attention to the proper regimen of his disease. He also likes fat women.

The little girl that mom attended to didn't like her new sitter. And to be fair to mom the kid was a little shit. One of those chubby blonde little girls that would run to her Daddy when he got home and begin to relay all the rotten things that Mrs. Duncan had done to her. Like feed her and make her wash. Mrs. Duncan made her clean up her room and do her homework. I couldn't believe the kid was talking about my Mom. I thought it was a hell of a coincidence that there was another lady working there that went by the name of Mrs. Duncan. The kid would whine and the doctor would soothe her.

The position of chief cook and bottle washer to the dentist and his spawn was not working out. The kid didn't like mom, mom didn't like the kid. So mom quit. All was not a loss, mom had met Jake. Unfortunately, Jake doesn't watch his diet and certainly doesn't watch his alcohol intake. Jake's diabetes has forced an amputation of his left leg.

* * *

A friend of the family worked for the federal government and offered mom a job. He told her what the job entailed and said that he would totally understand if she turned it down. She didn't turn it down and she went to work for the Government of Canada. Great pay, super benefits, weekends and holidays off, pension plan and a nice clean office downtown, not too far from the bus terminal.

I went over to congratulate her on landing a great job. We poured a couple of vodka tonics, I hadn't had rye since the time I stole a bottle and had puked my guts out. I sat at one end of the big yellow kitchen table and her at the other end. I proposed a toast to her success and then asked, "What is it that you do at the Post Office?"

"I don't work at the Post Office I work for Canada Customs."

"Oh, excuse me. So what exactly do you do at the customs office?" In my mind I pictured her tearing the back seat out of some kid's car searching for drugs. A snarling German Sheppard at her side. My inside voice said Not! "Well, I don't like to tell people the details of my work." This was a new tack for mom. Not talking about herself. "What are you involved in secret military operations." Why not I thought, it was the Federal Government she worked for. "No, I'm involved with the investigation of imported contraband. I decide what is acceptable to enter the country and what is to be turned back."

"How do you make that decision? What are the criteria for making such a decision?" I was floored, she works for the government for a week and now she's making policy? "Me and this guy sit in a room and watch movies and we decide what's okay to let in the country and what's not."

"Your censors?"

"Not really, we watch porno films." Unbelievable! "What are the rules? How does a movie get through?" "We have to agree or it doesn't get in."

"Well how many do you approve?"

"I approve a lot. As long as it doesn't involve children I pretty much let everything go. I'm not into the animal stuff but most of the rest is okay."

"And what about the other guy, what does he think?"

"He's a prude, he hardly lets anything pass."

* * *

With the new job came a new sense of independence. She was going to sell the house. She listed with a realtor friend who got

Mom to accept the first offer that came through the door. She signed for forty three thousand dollars. Now she was homeless.

I had been living in a walk up in a beautiful old building on James Street ever since Becky and I had separated. No one bothered me. I was within walking distance of every bar worth frequenting. I worked within walking distance of my apartment. For the head space I was occupying at the time it was a good fit. Mom could hardly wait to tell me that she was moving to an apartment not more than a block from my place. "Oh goody," was my response.

It was a modern building with a marble foyer and a gleaming glass elevator. Her suite was a spacious two bedrooms, two bathrooms, with a large living room, dining room and kitchen. Off the living room through a set of sliding glass doors was a balcony that overlooked a small park. It was a nice place. But that wasn't going to be enough for the new Olivia.

She commissioned two gay guys, Ron and Ron who were professional decorators, which meant that they overcharged for painting. They came in and took over her life and her bank account. They painted the entire apartment in a range of pastel greens and blues and a special mauve for her bedroom. They had green broadloom, it wasn't carpet, it was broadloom, throughout. In my mother's bedroom attached to the ceiling and surrounding her bed hung purple and mauve mosquito netting.

Large pictures of orchids with their stamens and pistils pointing vulgarly out in some erotic display intended purely to arouse an unsuspecting individual that might find himself trapped in this den of iniquity.

Elizabeth's bedroom was a pleasant blue with cornflower accents. A Louis the fourteenth head board gave the room a particularly historic ambiance

An old fashioned china wash basin and jug, decorated in a cornflower pattern, sat on an antique wash stand.

The living room was where Ron and Ron's talent came to the forefront. They spared none of my mother's expense in this room.

They had a settee custom built, it was just a box with some cushions on it and some arms fitted to it. The material was removable so that you had a winter set of coverings and a summer set of coverings. But that was not the best part, not by a long shot! The two Ron's had made kaftans for my Mother from the same material and patterns as the settee. Now she could blend into the room completely, regardless of what season it was. I never knew what purpose this internal camouflage served, unless of course you were going duck hunting in your living room.

Another of the decorating exclusives was the positioning of pictures throughout the room. Aside from the normal over the sofa type picture height you would find in any normal living room, Ron and Ron had hung pictures eight, twelve, maybe twelve and a half inches from the floor.

It started as you would come in the door. If you weren't careful you could kick the fruit right of the bowl of a pretty little still life that was hanging just inches above the baseboard. I suppose if you were drunk and passing out it would be a treat to admire the art work on the way down to the floor.

They furnished the balcony with rattan and enough candles to upset the eco system in the park next door. I always thought that twigs and fire were a nice combination to decorate in.

She loved it and she was happy. I suppose if investing twenty thousand dollars of you entire meager life savings into something that you didn't own and would never see any kind of return on was a wise move, then she was fucking brilliant.

* * *

It wasn't long after Ron and Ron had cashed their cheque that Mom informed Elizabeth that she would have to quit high school and get a job. Mom said she couldn't afford the tuition to Bishop Ryan High School, keep Elizabeth in bus fare, and feed her, 'There just wasn't enough money to go around." Elizabeth showed up at my apartment in tears. "Mom says we don't have enough money for me to keep going to school. I have to quit and get a job." All of us kids had gone to Bishop Ryan High School, some had even gone willingly. "Don't worry about a thing," I told her, "I'll go talk to mom and find out what's going on. You stay here and relax, have a beer or something. Beers the only soft drink I have. Unless you want scotch?" I walk over to Mom's apartment. She confirms what Elizabeth has told me. "I don't have enough money to keep Elizabeth at school."

"Well how much is the tuition?"

"It's three hundred dollars."

"Oh, so it's about the cost of one of these pillows I'm sitting on." As the words are leaving my mouth I have already realized the trap I have fallen into. I have opened the door, I am entering the void of dim-witted conversation. "You kids don't want me to have anything. I do one nice thing for myself and you want to deny me that."

"Look, let me pay the three hundred dollars and then Elizabeth can finish school. It's no big deal."

"It's not just the three hundred dollars, there's bus fare and food and"

"Stop it! With what that kid has been through with Dad and all I'm not going to let you fuck up her last year of school. She can come and live with me until she finishes school."

"Fine! You go ahead and see how easy it's going to be. You'll be pawning her off to me within a week."

I walk back to my apartment thinking that maybe that wasn't my brightest move. "Elizabeth, how would you like to move in here with me until your finished school?"

"I was hoping you would say that."

"You were?"

"Mom just rags on me all day about getting a job and how expensive everything is and how I don't help her. I hate it there."

"Oh." Says I.

So Elizabeth moves in. I give her money to go grocery shopping to buy stuff for her school lunches. She buys a bus pass. I give her money for her personal stuff. She says she doesn't need any personal stuff. I say, "You will." Oh my gosh, I'm thinking like a responsible parent. So that's what it feels like.

We carry on just fine. We don't get in each others way. I cook up some neat meals that we share every once in a while. Elizabeth works hard at school and at the end of the winter semester I have to sign her report card. We cook up some steaks out on the balcony to celebrate her good marks. I pretend that I'm Dad reviewing one of my report cards. The joke doesn't work and we both start crying. All and all it is a pretty neat experience for the both of us.

Mom starts to call for Elizabeth, lonely, she blames me. "It's a rotten thing that you have done, taking a daughter away from her mother." She starts in with her interpretation of events. "Well you practically kidnapped her. You're turning her against me." I guess the honeymoon with the apartment is over because she is back living on Fantasy Island. "Elizabeth can come home any time she wants to providing you let her finish high school. And you don't bug her about getting a job." Elizabeth and Mom have a girl to girl talk and she comes to me all teary eyed. "I think Mom is lonely. She wants me to move back with her. She says that she misses me. I think I had better move back with her."

"I think you should do whatever makes you happy. What do you want to do?" Elizabeth moves back to Mom's museum.

When Elizabeth moves back in with her mother she discovers that mom wasn't as lonely as perhaps she let on. Jake visits with Olivia quite regularly. He rolls his wheel chair through the plush broadloom as close to mom as the chrome and rubber chair will allow. Jake has given up both his legs to diabetes. He now quite literally doesn't have a leg to stand on.

A couple of weeks after Elizabeth has moved back in with her mother. Elizabeth shows up at my door, out of breath, eyes wide, half grin and total disbelief on her face. "I just walked in on Mom and Jake doing the deed on the living room floor." She breaks into hysterics, then stops, and then breaks into hysterics again. I'm laughing at her reaction. I haven't even begun to fathom the scene that my little sister has been exposed to. Elizabeth stands in the hallway bent over. She is laughing so hard the tears are dripping on to the floor.

Now I know from personal experience how hard it can be for a guy who is under pressure to put on his pants. If you are in a hurry it is difficult. You hop around on one foot while you try and insert your other leg into the pants. Once one leg is in you repeat the process only this time you are bent half way over at the waist until you can get it started in the other pant leg, then you pull them up. Everybody puts their pants on one leg at a time. Well everybody except Jake. The picture of Jake, frantically bouncing from bum cheek to bum cheek, his erect penis longer than his legs would make the pulling up of what little pants he had become a monumental task. "Can I stay here a little while?" "Are you kidding?"

WESTWARD ROLL THE WAGONS
ALWAYS WESTWARD ROLL,

It was time for me to depart. I had had enough. I was heading west. It was the time of Denver singing about getting high in the Rocky Mountains. There were people moving on to a simpler life style, back to nature. I was fed up with everyone and everything. I felt that I had done my duty and more. I believed that Alberta and the Rocky Mountains would just about be far enough away. Far enough away from this place that had taken so much out of me, far enough away to help heal my soul. Besides, there wasn't anything left to give. Whatever there had been was long gone and I intended it to be so with me.

Everybody in the family thought I was kidding until I loaded up my MG with whatever it would carry and drove away. I stopped at my Brothers on the way to say goodbye. We got loaded that night. In the morning he asked, "Well when are you coming back?"

"Never" was all I said and was gone.

* * *

Years later I took a road trip east to my Brother's home on Manitoulin Island. I love these long solitary drives. The brains secondary motor skills kick in almost as an auto pilot would on a long flight. Traveling down an interstate allows time to stand still and frees up the mind to enter a meditative state. A garden of thoughts spring up. As in a meditation, some thoughts you look at briefly and discard, some thoughts you explore and develop.

During one of these thought hikes I was following the path that all thoughts are tied together based on what we have experienced. If we cannot remember our experiences do we, or, can we think about our futures. A baby has no future thought because it has no experience to draw on. If a mind has lost the ability to remember does it also lose the power to look forward, to dream, to anticipate, to plan for the future? If we take away the promise of tomorrow, do we lose our capacity to think? As we continue to degenerate in our connections of forward thought do we begin to die? Having no tomorrow leaves us alone in today. In our most simplistic thoughts the sun will come up tomorrow. If we don't know that the sun will come up or for that matter, what the sun is and we have no understanding of the concept of tomorrow are we dying?

A baby's mind is developing, a diseased mind is dissolving. In a dissolving mind everything we have learned is unraveling, disintegrating, we are like an old star, collapsing into itself. In an Alzheimer's mind the process is quantifiable. We can watch, if we want to look, at a mind in reverse. The process takes about the same time as the baby's growth and into maturity. We just do not expect to see this process in our fathers, mothers, brothers and sisters. So we have ten years to watch a person we have loved, perhaps we have been married to them, enjoyed the falling in love, the physical and emotional relationship, the raising of children, the building of a life together. Perhaps it is a sibling.

* * *

Tooling along the highways I was anticipating our little family reunion. We had all agreed to meet on the island and spend some time together. Julie and Elizabeth were driving up from Hamilton and would walk on the ferry at Tobermory and James and I would drive down and pick them up at the ferry terminal on the south end of the island.

The afternoon was sunny and hot, they arrived to the smiling faces of their Brothers put there with the assistance of a few beers. We headed to James's boat where we had stocked additional booze and snacks for our cruise.

That night we sat around remembering and joking. Talking about all the shit we did as kids. The bean bat, the bedrooms, and the stunts we would pull to try and drive mom nuts. Elizabeth was quiet. I thought she may be a little nostalgic, although I could never understand why anybody would be missing those times. I always believed that we handled everything with humor in order to keep our sanity.

Finally she broke into the conversation with, "I want to thank you John for taking care of me when Mom wanted me to quit school. I don't think I have ever thanked you properly. Thank you, John." My sister took me by complete surprise. We hugged each other tightly.

The next day it was time to put the sisters back on the ferry. We arrived at the ferry landing. Elizabeth was confused and visibly upset. Elizabeth was unsure of her surroundings. She asked Julie why they were waiting to take a boat. Julie calmly explained that they had to get off the island because their car was on the other side and they needed to pick it up to get home.

In the months to follow it became clear to me the road that Elizabeth was headed down. All the sign posts were there, you just had to read them. You could avoid dealing with it. You could pretend that it wasn't happening. You could accept the doctors standing around scratching their heads and saying, "Well, we can't be sure?" I didn't need a diagnosis; I knew exactly what it was.

March 31, 2008

> *Dear Elizabeth,*
>
> *Your sister and bothers love you very much. It is because of this love we share for our youngest sister that I am writing to you.*
>
> *Last summer when we all got together on Manitoulin Island your brothers and sister noticed some behavioral changes in you. At times you were withdrawn, confused and unsure of your surroundings. Since that time I would surmise that these behaviors have become evident at your workplace resulting in the reason for your disability leave.*
>
> *You have told me that your medical advisers are treating you for depression and that is all well and good*

but there is another illness which symptoms can mimic those of depression and require a different regime of tests. That is Alzheimer's, particularly the early onset type.

Early Onset Familial Alzheimer's Disease occurs in about 5 percent of people afflicted with Alzheimer's and because of the onset in earlier years and it's similarities in symptoms to depression it is frequently miss-diagnosed by medical professionals. Determining the proper diagnosis saves precious time, time that can be spent with your family participating and enjoying life with all your loved ones. Let's not waste any precious time. Our family history needs to be shared with your medical professional and the proper tests conducted.

Elizabeth, what your sister and brothers are asking is for permission to be given us to either contact your doctors or attend a session in order that the family history be given and the appropriate steps are to be taken to eliminate all concerns. What we ask, we ask because we love you.

Love,
John

Acknowledgments

To my readers, Barbara, Arnold, Don, Michael, Susie and Ken. Thank you, your feedback and encouragement were appreciated.

Kevin, your help with the editing and formatting and your words of encouragement throughout the post project process were invaluable.

To the morning Beacon Coffee Clutch, thank you. Dependable and trustworthy, always. A special thanks to Richard for your technical assistance.

This book would not have seen the light of day if it were not for Carol. She who tills and toils in the meager soil of my mind and manages to help me grow. Thank you.

© Black Rose Writing

CPSIA information can be obtained at www.ICGtesting.com
Printed in the USA
LVOW120826040413

327469LV00003B/12/P